UNCOMPROMISING
INTIMACY

Turn Your Unfulfilling Marriage into
a Deeply Satisfying, Passionate Partnership

ALEXANDRA STOCKWELL MD

DISCLAIMER

Throughout this book I have used examples from many of my clients personal lives. However, to ensure privacy and confidentiality, I have changed their names and some of the details of their experiences. None of the personal examples of my own life have been altered.

Praise For
Uncompromising Intimacy

What I love about this book is it gives couples hope. In my work and in life, I too often hear people giving up on finding love, passion and deep fulfillment with their partner and decide that it must not be possible with "this" person. *Uncompromising Intimacy* can breathe life back into your relationship and set you on a path to manifest a deep connection. You CAN have what you want in your relationship. Alexandra provides the keys in these pages that can unlock the love, romance and partnership you desire.

JJ Flizanes, Author of Fit 2 Love and
Host of Spirit Purpose & Energy Podcast
Los Angeles, CA

Dr. Stockwell's accessible and informative book should be mandatory reading for anyone in a relationship. The blueprint she provides to rekindle and fortify a relationship is communicated openly, grounded in Dr. Stockwell's own experience. Her method works, and is vital to help our society learn to relate to others, communicate with our loved ones, and live life in a more deeply fulfilling manner.

Pamela Adelstein, MD
Newton, MA

This book is a gem! Whether you've been with your partner for one month or 50 years, you will love this book. It is a quick read filled with so many profound ideas and tools that you will want to read it multiple times. It is a very practical guide to the path of greater peace, joy, and passion in your relationship. My partner and I have been using these principles for years in our relationship and we still found so many pearls of wisdom in this book that I now recommended this book to all my friends.

Jerry Gould, DC
Wenham, MA

With *Uncompromising Intimacy* Dr Stockwell has created a much-needed system to help the silent majority of relationships. This isn't a book just for those in crisis. This book is for those in tolerable to good relationships who want to reignite the spark and find the passion they know they and their partner deserve. This is a wonderful book that will help improve the lives inside and outside of the sheets for many couples.

Elliot Roe, High Performance Coach,
Salt Lake City, Utah

Uncompromising Intimacy is a powerful combination of experience, solutions and heartfelt connective expressions, and it's written in a relatable yet potent style. Alexandra's simple but clear descriptions helped me move through the book with hope, while making an indelible imprint on my mind and heart. I will take much of what I learned directly into my relationships.

Tim Taylor,
Start Up and Business Development Executive
San Francisco, CA

This book is an absolute gift for couples and individuals aspiring to create connected and passionate long-term partnerships.

I have already recommended this book to each of my clients and most of my friends. It's one to read multiple times, and its length is perfect in order to effortlessly prioritize doing so regularly.

Antesa Jensen, Emotional Intelligence Expert,
Copenhagen, Denmark

I am so inspired by Alexandra's story and how she practices what she teaches. Her experience and wisdom is clearly evident and the process she teaches is simple yet so profound. I felt like I was being gently guided into a deep space of healing in partnership. I felt the possibility of being able to have the type of relationship she wrote about. I also loved how easy the book was to read because of her elegant yet direct writing style.

Po-Hong Yu, LAc
New York, NY

Alexandra Stockwell's relationship wisdom shines from each and every page of this delightful book.

With clarity, examples, and powerful tools and techniques, she leads the reader into deep and loving insights to manifest the best partnerships possible.

Barbara Wayman, PR Professional,
Columbus, Ohio

Alexandra has a way of bringing awareness to intimacy and improving your relationships with ease. Her nature of acceptance and willingness to speak about what really matters stands out in this book! Love her style and voice. If you are looking for a book to improve your relationship and practical ways to realize success, this book is for you!

Teresa Lodato, Relationship Coach,
Pleasanton, CA

Dr. Stockwell's portrait of a committed relationship as an infinite, renewable source of growth is sexy, and one from which everyone will benefit. She reveals the blueprint for how we can change our relationships, our families, and our world. Take her journey, it's worth the ride.

Susan Kahn, Attorney,
New York, NY

Dedication

For Rodd, with all my love.

For our children Josephine, Christopher, Gabriel and Matthew--this book is here for you when you want to read it.

For couples everywhere who want passionate, deeply connected relationships.

Table of Contents

CHAPTER 1

Is the Comfort of Companionship as Good as It Gets?

❦

- Is it possible to experience ongoing emotional intimacy and sensual passion in a long-term relationship?

- Will we be able to sustain our erotic connection?

- Can we create a fantastic sex life, even if we never had one to begin with?

These questions plague many couples; couples who love one another deeply. They whisper in the background when you yearn to feel intimate connection with your beloved, when you yearn to feel cherished and adored. And the questions simmer to the surface as you want to be supported in becoming the best version of yourself. You also want to be the kind of person who offers this quality of connection to your partner. But you can't figure out how.

Maybe you have read a number of books on how to improve your relationship, or how to improve yourself. Maybe you have done therapy at one point or another, experiencing short-term benefits which didn't last. Maybe you don't really know what you want anymore, because it feels too hard to figure it out. And if you did know, you wouldn't know how to create it anyway. Yet you are absolutely certain that you both want to stay together, so it really is worthwhile to figure out how to enjoy one another more.

These mostly unspoken challenges linger in the air, silently. You only really notice them in the rare moments you are alone, or when you look through old photographs and feel an ache for rekindled connection. Or perhaps you feel jealous when you see a friend from college in a happy flirtatious photo with her husband while on vacation. You want so badly to feel how she feels, to have what she appears to have. Mostly though, you don't let these thoughts derail you because there is so much good in your life. You and your partner are devoted to your family, to the raising of your children, and to providing for all their needs. For the most part, you don't doubt that he's the right partner for you.

Even so, you aren't happy, and you can't figure out what to do about it.

First of all, let me tell you that you are not alone, far from it!

As a society, we are collectively struggling in our attempts to build lasting relationships. The divorce rate is staggeringly high as is the huge percentage of couples who are dissatisfied with the quality of their relationship.

While maintaining a relationship is obviously challenging, this book is *not* about staying together. It is for you, because you *do* want to stay together. You and your partner are committed, and the question is *not* about *whether* to stay together. It is *how*!

- *How* do you co-create a relationship that fulfills your true yearning, one that doesn't just look good on the outside, but truly feeds your soul?

- *How* do you create a relationship that fuels your purpose, and brings delight and play to every day?

2

- *How* do you create a relationship with both planned and spontaneous adventures to places you want to visit?

- *How* do you create a relationship where you feel the solidity that comes with knowing someone well, plus the delight that comes with discovering new things, having new experiences, and learning more about your partner?

The problem of *how* is completely understandable. Because as mammals, one of the primary ways we learn is through imitation. But when we look around for great long-term relationships worthy of emulation, we come up very short. And when we don't have strong imprinting, it's hard to know *how*.

When I first became a relationship coach, early in working with a couple, I used to ask them whom they admired. What were the relationships that inspired them and motivated them – either in their own family, or in their extended network of friends and acquaintances, or in movies, literature, or celebrities. Every time the couple would look at one another, wondering, and come up empty. I never had anyone answer the question with clarity and conviction so eventually I stopped asking. In the process I learned much about the lack of role-model couples along with the huge need for them.

This isn't to say that there aren't people who really admire the love their parents or grandparents share. But that doesn't mean it is the relationship they want to be experiencing. Times change rapidly with the generations and what worked for your grandparents is unlikely to work for you. Consider how gender roles are different, women's relationship to work and purpose has changed, and our expectations of what we will experience in a marriage has evolved. What that means is that we have an overload of examples of long-term committed relationships which are not what we are looking for, and a dearth of those that would be worthwhile aspiring to. In other words, we lack a roadmap, or as I like to say, a blueprint for the kind of relationship we yearn for.

The research is consistent with this dilemma: While the divorce rate is high, the data on those who stay together is equally discouraging. Actually, we don't have very much data because there are few entities who fund such research. When it comes to incidence and patterns of disease, or even education, there are many corporations that see financial benefit in collecting data, but that isn't true when it comes to relationships. One exception to this is Durex, the condom maker. As part of a study, the Durex company interviewed 29,000 couples and found that 54 percent were dissatisfied with the quality of their relationships. Other research has shown that up to 84 percent of married couples aren't happy with the intimacy they experience.

In working with couples, I have discovered that there are three main kinds of relationships: *toxic, termination*, and *toleration:*

A toxic relationship is one in which fear and anger govern most interactions. This can involve violence and abuse of various kinds. A toxic relationship doesn't have a safe enough container to do the work in this book. If you are reading this book and that is your situation, I encourage you to turn to another resource for support and return to this book when your relationship is more stable.

In a termination relationship, one or both people have already given up on the relationship. Maybe you have already filed for divorce, or perhaps you are waiting to do so for one reason or another. There are often significant financial reasons to stay together, or you need psychological stability and are not ready to rock the boat. In fact, one in four couples stay together until all the children are out of the house; they stay together for the sake of the children even though they would otherwise separate. If you are in a termination relationship, there will be valuable material for you in this book which you can use to improve the mood in your home. You will learn how to co-parent and co-create with your spouse in a way that is more satisfying for both of you. However, the promise of this book – to show you the path to create emotional intimacy and passionate, deeply satisfying sex, is for readers who are in relationships where *both* of you are committed to the relationship and willing to do what it takes to make it fantastic.

If you are, in fact, committed to making the relationship work, you may be in the third kind of relationship, the toleration relationship. The vast majority of couples are in toleration relationships. These are relationships where they have learned to live with things that don't feel great and don't really work for them, but they are overriding their unmet needs and desires in order to save the relationship.

In the toleration relationship, there is no question whether you love each other, because you really do. Furthermore, there are countless things you love about the life you have built together. You can depend on one another to show up for your children, to be punctual to important events, to do your best to provide for your family, and to be there for each other most of the time. But, despite all of this felt love and evidence of commitment, your life together feels relatively stale, mundane, and unfulfilling. It might be painful to admit, because in a toleration relationship the hurt is often buried deep below the surface. In fact it's important to you that your relationship looks good on the outside; you don't want to trouble your kids and you certainly don't want others to think there is anything wrong. You may think to yourself that so many other couples deal with much bigger problems, so why focus on what isn't working.

In a toleration relationship, you are likely to be personally and professionally competent, and it throws you off to discover any sense of incompetence when it comes to intimate relating. You don't want to deal with it and may have put off acknowledging it to anyone, even to yourself. Instead you put more time and energy into your work, or a volunteer project, or working out, or pursuing a new hobby, or making yoga and meditation a regular commitment. You engage with *anything* that takes you away from directly facing what isn't working.

You have probably, at some point, tried bringing this up with your partner, but it never goes well. You don't feel heard and it's not satisfying. Typically, he ends up defensive and blaming, or completely withdrawn, which leaves you even more frustrated than before.

So instead, in the evening, after dinner is cleaned up and the kids are set with their homework, you watch Netflix and fall asleep, or you read your own book and give him a peck on the cheek before turning out the light. It's not satisfying, but it works.

In this kind of relationship, you are part of the majority of couples that talk about something other than kids and logistics for less than four minutes a day. There is no talk of your dreams, your desires for the future, new insights about life. Instead, you stick to the topics that are straightforward and emotionally uncomplicated, except every now and then when you can't contain it and express your emotions in an intense jumble. All of a sudden, you share much of what isn't working for you. The result is that your partner is thrown off guard, and you end up back where you started from, waiting for the sting to lessen once again. I often describe this kind of relationship as "conflict-free and passion-free".

At first glance, especially from the outside, "conflict-free" might look pretty good. And I am certainly not an advocate of conflict for conflict's sake. But if you turn down the volume on what matters to you in everyday life, papering things over to keep the peace, and compromising on things that are important, you end up sacrificing more than you ever meant to. Avoiding topics because they will be awkward or unpleasant means you are holding yourself back, and abandoning your own soul for the sake of the relationship. Inevitably, if you compromise in your daily life on a regular basis, it is very challenging to dial things back up and bring all of yourself forward when it's time for passion and sensual communion in the bedroom.

We are whole beings and when we numb ourselves, override our needs, ignore our desires, neutralize our yearnings, and withhold our truest feelings on a regular basis, we don't have easy access to them in times of passion and intimate self-expression.

This is where *The Blueprint For Conscious Partnership* comes in. It shows you the way to cultivate the fourth kind of relationship: The Conscious Partnership.

In conscious partnership, you and your partner treat your relationship as the vehicle for personal transformation. You learn to bring all of yourselves to the relationship, learning to love who you are and accept all of who your partner is. This naturally leads to erotic intimacy, hot sex, soul stirring passion, and the knowledge you need to continue to expand from that juncture into the rest of your life.

There aren't too many couples who have cracked the code and live true conscious partnership, and those that do aren't always forthcoming about it because the experience is intimate, sacred, and often private. Even so, there is a growing revolution of couples who are transforming how they relate to one another. They are consistently accessing new depths of satisfaction with one another, and finding joy and satisfaction emotionally and sensually. Reading this book is your next step to becoming one of those couples!

Exercise

- Get pen and paper, and write a page or two in response to the following questions:

- What kinds of relationships did your parents and other main role models have?

- Were they toxic relationships, characterized by anger and fear?

- Were they termination relationships, with divorce or separation while living under the same roof?

- Did the relationships have qualities of toleration, where each of them held back parts of who they were and what they needed, in order to maintain the status quo?

- Or were you one of the rare children who grew up with one or more parents in a conscious partnership, wherein self-expression, sovereignty, emotional intimacy and passionate connection were the norm?

- What insights do you have into your own relationship after writing your responses to the previous questions?

CHAPTER 2

My Journey from Physician to Relationship and Intimacy Expert

During orientation week for the University of Massachusetts Family Medicine Residency Program, I participated in an exercise that was part of a cultural sensitivity training we were required to attend. We had patients from almost every country in the world who came to our clinic and it was important that we knew how to interact with them respectfully. In that training I learned *not* to show our Vietnamese and Cambodian patients the bottom of my shoe because it was equivalent to giving them the middle finger. I learned that Albanian patients often shake their head side to side when they mean "yes" and up and down when they mean "no." It was a remarkable training that was designed to give me the tools to be respectful in the ways I wanted to be but, without the training, wouldn't have known how.

Part of the cultural sensitivity training involved some self-reflection and personal identification of the cultures we ourselves had grown up in. This was important for clarifying the lens through which each of us perceived the world and the people in it. One of my classmates was half Venezuelan, another came from working class Polish roots. I come from a dynamic line of New York Jews, including a great-grandfather from Hungary who supported his family of twelve beginning when he was a young teenager, and my grandfather who

9

walked from Moscow to Germany and never went back as the rest of his family was killed when the Bolsheviks came to power. It includes two grandmothers who were college educated in the 1920s and 1930s, a father who went to MIT when he was sixteen and a mother who was part of creating interdisciplinary academics in the 1960s at Pembroke before it became Brown. My family traditions and cuisine are fascinating, quirky, intellectual, and soulful. Yet, that wasn't what came up for me that day. As I went through the exercise I realized my tribe, my primary *cultural identity,* came from being a child of divorce. When I meet someone whose parents divorced in the elementary school years, I feel kinship and understanding. I feel a sense of commonality and a wordless sense of shared perspective. I hadn't known that before participating in the training, but once I did, so much of my inner life made sense to me.

At the time I realized all of this, I had been with my husband for seven years, married for four, and we had a three-year-old girl and a one-year-old boy. By all appearances, we were a lovely young family with two parents who were physicians in residency training. And indeed, that was true, unequivocally true. We supported one another. We collaborated on the logistics involved in raising two children, running a household, and working sixty to a hundred hours a week, and we did so relatively cheerfully, and with a deep sense of companionship.

However, despite living collaboratively, starting from our very first moments of parenthood, I simultaneously enjoyed our new life together *and* told myself we would get divorced. I used to make a mental note to tell my daughter what a devoted father she had. I imagined telling her this when she was older, and we were divorced, and she would no longer be able to see how mutually supportive we once had been in our marriage. I wanted to hold that image for her, knowing that it wouldn't be that way in the future.

10

After all, my mother had remarried and divorced again. After a number of longterm girlfriends, my father married a woman who had already been twice married and divorced. On top of this, my husband's parents had divorced when he was six. Given our combined family legacy, I was too intelligent to ever just assume Rodd and I would stay together; my unconscious conditioning had taught me that divorce was inevitable since it is what I grew up with and all I had ever known. So there I was participating in a marriage that seemed wonderful, and actually *was* wonderful, even as I fundamentally doubted its reliability.

Both my husband and I had had good experiences with individual therapy before we met, and I wanted to give our relationship the same attention, the same opportunity for internal exploration, improved awareness, and the space to discover more about ourselves. Therefore, from the time we were serious about one another, I knew it would be wonderful to have couples coaching or therapy and I looked forward to doing so well before our relationship was in crisis.

In the late 1990s, in Boston, we attended a communication workshop for couples and then signed up for therapy with the facilitator. After a few sessions, we decided to use the time with the therapist just for me; it had become apparent that many of the challenges in our relationship were resulting from my childhood wounds, wounds I needed to heal for myself and for the sake of our relationship.

Throughout our relationship, starting soon after we began to date, people would express admiration for how we were with one another. This was even happening around the time we started counseling. People would tell us that they wanted a relationship like ours because we were kind to one another and because we really did get

11

along well! I believe the reason we got along so well and felt truly connected, even in the midst of raising young children, working long hours, and having an unconscious pull towards divorce, was the result of our Sunday evening conversations.

Every Sunday evening we used to spend two or three hours with our calendars in hand, figuring out how the week would work, who would cook dinner, and which one of us would be available if our children were sick or our nanny was unavailable.

Those Sunday evening conversations had a practical purpose and they also were the context in which we learned to be considerate of one another, speaking up for our own needs, and looking for the win-win for both of us and our family as a whole.

Our early years together were filled with working hard, lots of exams, little sleep, with each of us having thirty-six-hour shifts on a regular basis, not to mention bringing babies into the world and caring for them. We really didn't have time then to nurture the passionate side of our relationship. We didn't go out on dates and we aimed to derive our share of joy from spending time with our children.

It worked for us. We had the same values. We were devoted to our marriage, our children, and our careers, and we felt the strength and comfort of mutual support. We made love but it was never long hours of bliss where we got lost in one another's souls or bodies. In fact, our therapist described our connection as strong and lush in the upper chakras, and mostly underdeveloped in the lower chakras. We recognized this as true as soon as he said it.

We continued this way, with one or both of us occasionally yearning for more, but also really satisfied with the life we were building.

By the mid-2000s, I had been in medicine for twelve years. I had my own small practice in Massachusetts, and I loved being a doctor. We had been married for ten years, and had three of our four children. I thought, at the time, that I should have some sense of having *arrived*. After all, I had everything I had striven for: a stable marriage, a healthy family, and a meaningful career. But instead of a sense of fulfillment, of feeling really great about accomplishing my goals, I felt a hollowness inside. It felt uncomfortable, like something should be there that wasn't.

In addition, around this time, both of my parents died. In the wake of those deaths, and the 2008 downturn in the housing market which resulted in an enormous loss for us, everything in my life that had heretofore felt stable, suddenly felt like it was coming apart. I had expected to live in Massachusetts and practice medicine for many more decades. Now, that was questionable. I didn't know how I wanted to live anymore and wasn't even sure what I meant when I said so. In reality, everything in my life was up in the air except my devotion to my marriage and our children.

During this time period, I also found that I prioritized my patients needs over my family's, and my family's needs over my own. I tried time management techniques, a vision board, and various other suggestions I encountered. I worked with a healer on self worth and did everything I could to transform this tendency; I still found myself stuck, taking care of everyone else and living with priorities that I didn't actually align with, despite knowing better. Simply put I couldn't figure out how to put my own oxygen mask on first. It's worth noting that I was not explicitly suffering, nor was anyone else in my family, but I could see the path ahead. I knew if nothing changed I would inevitably end up feeling depleted and resentful. I knew it was unsustainable and didn't want to continue living that way.

Around this time, my daughter Josephine turned nine. The day of her birthday she was her usual radiant, warm, self-expressed, feminine self. She was beautiful. And ... her being that way caught me off guard and freaked me out. I hid my response from others but it was very, very intense for me. My reaction was a direct response to not being able to relate to how magnificent she was.

I immediately thought of myself at nine, when my parents got divorced. At that time I began to turn inward, withdraw emotionally, and turn to food for comfort. I no longer trusted that the adults around me would take good care of me as they were attuned to their own big processes as they moved through divorce and then life after divorce. In a split second, I contrasted who I was at nine to who my daughter was at nine; I couldn't relate to her radiance and that hit me hard. In that moment, I realized that I had never truly regained the joy and delight in life that had been suppressed by painful circumstances so many years before.

As a physician with a focus on psychology and child development, I know all too well that children learn all kinds of things from their parents. I realized, that despite being a competent, warm, and loving mother, that if I was not truly in touch with my own joy and delight in being alive, it wouldn't be possible for my daughter to sustain her radiance for another nine years of living at home. It would be too hard for her to do so in the face of my dialed-down vibrancy. Honestly, I had never thought of myself as having a dialed-down presence because I laughed often and enjoyed my life. But in that moment, I saw that I had disconnected from the pleasure of being a woman, of having a female body; I had cut myself off from being a radiant, feminine woman.

More easily motivated to shift for my daughter's benefit than my own, I went all in. I enrolled in classes at the *School of Womanly*

Arts in New York. I also took dance classes and did spiritual trainings. I participated in high energy, transformative personal growth trainings and learned to be spontaneous, fun, and a little unpredictable, all while continuing to be a responsible, devoted mother at home.

As I explored what would have me feel alive, vibrant, sexy, and filled with pleasure, I decided to explore my own sensuality and sexuality as well. This was extremely unexpected because it hadn't ever been a huge focus for me. I wasn't a prude, not at all. But sex was never a major focus either. After all, my mother never discussed sex with me until I had had two children. My early education regarding sexuality came from women's magazines in my dentist's office. I remember reading a quiz in *Good Housekeeping* when I was in fifth grade. The quiz included a question about how many times a woman had sex with her husband in the course of a month. I was astonished. I had had no idea that adults had sex because it was enjoyable. I had thought they only did so in order to make babies!

So there I was, in my early forties, exploring sensuality and sexuality in depth for the very first time. One of my first adventures was dancing burlesque in a club in lower Manhattan. It was completely different than anything I had ever done before. It felt positively surreal, and I enjoyed it because I felt so alive while doing it.

Over the next few years, I participated in some pleasant educational workshops, and then, with growing courage, I moved on to edgier workshops, where the teachings would be shocking for a mainstream audience. This was before *Shades of Gray*, and before porn was prolific on the internet, so I truly had no frame of reference for what I was learning.

Every time I showed up at a training, I was the only person there who was married, with children, and living the life of a busy professional in the suburbs. My classmates tended to be young, in a phase of finding themselves, or living a polyamorous life with multiple partners, or exploring their kinky fetishes. Literally, no one else was going home after a weekend intensive to make dinner for a family with three kids and two cars, to make sure homework was completed before Monday morning, and to pack lunches and line up the backpacks.

Those trainings were an amazing opportunity for me. I had been comfortable with bodies and bodily activities from clinical experiences as a physician, but I was, at least initially, quite uneasy facing the intensity of passion. I was uncomfortable and unnerved by so much erotic energy and witnessing the edges people push when devoted to cultivating its development. In those experiences, I learned to see the humanity in people and in their sexuality. Simultaneously I learned to accept the erotic in all the myriad ways it presents. My comfort zone stretched and expanded as I integrated the erotic energy and brought home what I learned while participating in edgy experiences; I discovered how to transpose them into my marital life with Rodd. In fact, once I let go of judgment and stopped being controlling, I accessed a multitude of orgasmic energy and erotic passion.

One of my most triumphant moments involved learning how to playfully and authentically bring my erotic energy into our home, while simultaneously nurturing my children and mothering with care. As a first step I got rid of my monotone, shapeless aprons, and purchased a super cute French maid's apron that was also functional. I wore that sweet item whenever I cooked dinner and it made my time in the kitchen quite enjoyable.

While my family sat at the dinner table, I researched what happened when my attention was on my children's table manners and making sure everyone did what they were supposed to do, while also orienting to my husband as the hot sexually attractive man he is. I compared that to what happened when I focused on my children's behavior while viewing my husband as a partner in parenting. I also explored the outcome when I didn't have any attention on him at all.

The results were astonishing. When I brought my attention to my own erotic feelings, breathed more deeply, spoke more slowly, and intentionally swirled my hips, I noticed that my husband was more engaged in our dinnertime conversations, and all four children were calmer and more emotionally satisfied.

As I noticed this, I was heartened. I suddenly saw that the best way to serve my children was to have a great relationship with their father. Likewise the best way for me to serve all children is to teach their parents how to have hot, passionate, connected relationships. When parents enjoy themselves in this way, it both provides the gift of modeling something that will serve the children in the future, and it makes the present more satisfying and developmentally nourishing.

Once I was clear that claiming my delight as a woman and learning how to have passionate sex with my husband was going to be fantastic for me, feed our marriage and deepen our love, and also serve our children now and in the future, it became the primary focus of my life.

It was easier said than done, because cultivating great sex in long-term relationships requires a conscious and sustainable approach that is wholly different then what takes place in new relationships, casual flings, or one-night stands. In long-term relationships, deeply satisfying erotic passion requires honesty and vulnerability. It is essential to speak the truth, and that especially applies to truths that have been withheld a long time.

With new eagerness, my husband and I made sure to spend more time together, took care with how we spoke with one another, paid more attention to how we treated one another, and we courageously brought a new focus to our experiences while intimately touching one another. Sometimes it was frustrating and we would slink away, hurt and resentful, and wondering if it would ever improve. Other times, we would stop in the midst of lovemaking that was frustrating, and burst out laughing at ourselves, acknowledging how hard we were trying to do something which was meant to be pleasurable. Yet, slowly but surely, we learned to create blissful ecstasy, through touching each other's bodies and souls as we had never done before. We learned to extend our lovemaking for hours, to enjoy silently devouring one another so as not to wake kids, and to take advantage of a midday moment when we were alone in the house, filling the space with a variety of moans, squeals of delight, and unbridled ecstasy.

Drawing on my medical training, research done by therapists and other relationship coaches, what I have learned from hundreds of clients, and my own experience with my husband of twenty-four years, I have created *The Blueprint for Conscious Partnership*. I have taught it to other couples so they can create their own version of this kind of relationship. Because after all, in the context of long-term committed relationships, everything which isn't sex can be considered foreplay.

Exercise

- On a long piece of paper (or a few regularly sized ones taped together), using colored pencils, markers, or whatever you have nearby, make a timeline of the important events in your relationship. Include significant milestones, as well as meaningful internal shifts. Include births, deaths, moves, career advancements or setbacks, as well as noteworthy conversations, defining moments, times of fulfillment and times of real hurt.

- What do you notice when you look at your timeline?

- Take some time to journal about your observations and insights, and if you wish, when you are finished, share them with your partner.

CHAPTER 3
Passion and Pleasure Are Possible

I used to wonder if it was possible to create a great marriage that would endure through the ups and downs of life. I had good reason to wonder this. First of all, the national divorce statistics made my question exceedingly reasonable: fifty percent of first marriages, sixty percent of second marriages, and seventy-three percent of third marriages end in divorce. Consider too, that twenty-five percent of couples stay together for the sake of their children alone. Technically, they are together, but neither one actually *wants* to be with the other.

My own parents divorced after fourteen years of marriage, at the end of my third grade year. At the time I was attending a Waldorf School in a suburb of New York City. Eighteen months later, when I was in fifth grade, my teacher returned from Christmas vacation having gotten divorced himself. Another student's parents also divorced that month, which resulted in my suddenly being in the majority, with more than half the students in my class having divorced parents. With all of this personal and statistical evidence, I naturally wondered if it was possible to create a great marriage, and if it was possible, how did it happen? Was it some kind of lucky miracle or was it something else? How could I find out?

My great-grandparents were married in the early 1900s and my great-grandmother, Nana Ethel, used to say that she cried every day for the first ten years of her marriage. She then went on to have the happiest and best marriage of anyone she knew. While I was glad she had no regrets and came to adore my intense, intellectual, fiery New York attorney great-grandfather even though she herself was mild-mannered and loved poetry and soft fabrics, that model of marriage did not appeal to me. I couldn't see crying every day for ten years in order to earn my "happily ever after."

I looked around me and didn't find any relationship that truly inspired me in my own family, in my friends' families, among celebrities, even in literature or movies. I guess I liked a few of the wonderful characters in Broadway musicals, but as I grew up, and was in my early twenties, I was wise enough to know that being married was not easy and doing it well didn't come naturally to anyone I had encountered.

There were, of course, people who were very happily married but none of them had a relationship that I wanted to emulate. I didn't want to have to live as though it were one hundred years earlier, or even thirty, in order to participate in a model of marriage conducive to sustained happiness. For me, fulfillment has to include being a modern woman with a career. It also has to include pursuing a lot of interests beyond what I perceived in the stereotypical 1950s housewife. As a young woman, I couldn't bear to imagine building a life around having dinner ready when my future husband arrived home from work. It sounded antiquated to me, extremely boring, and far too much unpleasant, hard work.

Years later, when I began coaching couples, I routinely asked them to tell me about other couples in relationships they admired and none of them *ever* had an answer, not one! They were fairly clear on so much that *didn't* work for them, but when I asked them to imagine what they *did* want, and how they wanted to *feel* with each other, they very quickly fell back into naming what they didn't want, or began to detail a kind of unrealistic Disney- style fantasy where the woman is miserable and incomplete, but once rescued by a man is instantaneously fulfilled. And of course, everyone lives happily ever after.

So eventually I stopped asking clients that question.

But the question remained alive within me:

Is it possible to create an amazing relationship, wherein each person grows without sacrificing important aspects of who they are? A relationship wherein *together* they are unquestionably more alive, more vibrant, and more true to themselves precisely because they are together? Could a relationship exist where the bond is not only rooted in raising children, shared bank accounts, and a shared address, but grounded in something much deeper?

If it was possible, I knew it would mean one partner counting on the other to tell the truth, especially truths that the person wasn't yet seeing on their own. This might mean calling out shadow qualities and feelings causing shame. However, it is just as likely that it would mean revealing unacknowledged greatness and articulating superpowers, because both kinds of qualities are typically more apparent to a woman's partner than they are to her.

I imagined that this kind of connection would be one where sensuality and sexuality continuously deepen, and become more exquisite over time. It would include stability, comfort and companionship, the foundation of a partnership where both people rely on one another with rock-solid certainty. In addition, the couple would welcome new experiences, and look forward to exploring inner landscapes and outer terrain. Sensuality, eroticism, and sexuality would become more and more pleasurable. Life together would be a fulfilling and fortifying adventure.

I was eager to know: is it possible to have a truly mature, dynamic, sensual, intimate relationship with the person you marry and build a life with for decades to come? I remember thinking that if I cracked the code for my own marriage, I definitely would want to guide others to their own unique version of a fulfilling, deeply satisfying, passionate relationship.

Well, I am writing this book because I *finally* answered the question. And, in case you were wondering, yes it is absolutely possible!

Based on scientific research, my experience as a physician and as a coach guiding countless men and women in their relationships, and from what I have learned in my own marriage of twenty-four years, I created the *Blueprint For a Conscious Partnership.*

As mentioned before, a conscious partnership is one where both partners treat the relationship as a vehicle for personal transformation, where both people learn to bring all of who they are into the relationship and learn to love and be loved for exactly that.

A conscious partnership defies the age-old teaching that successful marriage requires compromise. In fact, as a wife to my husband Rodd of twenty-four years, a mother of four, and a coach to hundreds, I believe the key to passion, fulfillment, intimacy, and success in relationships isn't compromise, it's being *unwilling* to compromise. Because when people feel free to be themselves, and know how to love and be loved for exactly who they are, relationships are juicy, nourishing, and deeply satisfying.

This book provides the roadmap for conscious partnership. It is written with the understanding that almost everyone has grown up influenced personally, and in society at large, by one of the three types of relationships discussed in a previous chapter (toxic, termination, and toleration). It is unlikely that readers would be intimately familiar with conscious partnerships because once again, we simply do not have role models. I want to be a mentor to you and provide a roadmap so that you can create a beautiful conscious partnership with your current partner, regardless of your childhood conditioning.

Conscious partnership is co-created through embodying six essential qualities. The six essential qualities are:

- Cultivate Curiosity

- Embrace Honesty

- Be Kind

- Choose Happiness

- Take Responsibility

- Seek Growth

Each of the subsequent chapters delves into detail on how to embody one of the qualities. They are all fairly easy to conceptually understand although they require steadfast attention to implement them well. Together they constitute an invitation to engage with yourself and others in a meaningful way that is best done as a lifelong practice.

A *practice* is something which is done on a regular basis, and over time proficiency and mastery are achieved. This book is your invitation to begin! If you are further along on your personal development journey, take the opportunity to deepen your awareness and up-level your practice. It's time to learn new tools as well as to hone your embodiment of the qualities with which you're already familiar.

The six qualities of conscious partnership are intellectually distinct, and I write about them separately, but each one is an aspect of the essence of conscious partnership. Each quality interacts with the others holographically, and whichever quality you start with will pave the way to strengthen subsequent ones.

While any order would do, I start with "cultivate curiosity." It is the easiest quality to embody because it requires a relatively small amount of effort and it generates significant positive short and long-term benefits. Naturally, that's very encouraging and creates forward momentum.

Although each of the six qualities is interwoven with the others, I highly recommend you work on them in the sequence I wrote them. Pace yourself, and create a foundation of warmth and curiosity before you tread in more confronting waters, such as sharing vulnerable truths.

As you read further you are sure to have insights and awareness about yourself, your partner, and the dynamics between you. I encourage you to focus on your own growth and share with him what you are discovering about yourself. This is not a time for blame. Don't tell him your new accounting of how he shows up, and the way his shortcomings contribute to your pain. Instead focus on creating a foundation of lifelong transformation and sustainable, erotic heat.

As you read this, please know that I appreciate your willingness to look closely at your relationship. In my mind whatever your current situation, it's not good or bad, and it's not right or wrong. It is just how it has been. That's true whether your sex is beautiful but infrequent, or it's dissatisfying, and/or you can't remember the last time you made love, or perhaps you remember exactly when it was and are counting the days, weeks, and now months until it happens again. Either way, I invite you to let go of any self-criticism or judgment, and any kind of comparison. Instead, as you read this book, observe your own process with openness and curiosity.

You may be eager to improve your relationship, or you may be skeptical, even jaded, about what is possible for you. Perhaps you have worked with a couple's therapist and experienced some short-term improvement before things slipped back to how they were. That's quite common. In fact, seventy per cent of traditional couple's therapy is unsuccessful. However, I believe that to be the result of the training most couples therapists receive. It typically equips them to do conflict resolution and crisis intervention. However, for the majority of couples, conflict resolution is not what is needed. In fact in my practice, the majority of my clients are couples with relatively little conflict in their relationship. Instead, they have what I have already described as *conflict-free, passion-free relationships*.

Couples in this type of relationship have learned to set things aside, brush them under the rug, or ignore them and put their attention elsewhere. The problem with this is that when you withhold in some areas of your life, you can't help but withhold in others. So if you tend to compromise or acquiesce or choose some other flavor that minimizes conflict in your relationship and you are doing this on a day to day basis, everyday for years, it's quite likely that when you are in the bedroom you will be turned off and suppress there too. In this context, traditional therapy has little to contribute.

The six qualities of conscious partnership provide a blueprint for you to bring *all* of yourself into your relationship, to transition from compromising to being uncompromising. Instead of avoiding conflict and consequently inadvertently dialing down passion too, you will learn how to be more present with yourself and your partner, how to feel your feelings and share them responsibly, with vulnerability and connection. And therein lies the key to move from a sexless and affection-starved marriage to one where you are cherished and adored.

The chapters that follow will teach you ways of being that naturally result in you feeling seen and supported by the one you love best, with both of you knowing how to create and maintain a sensual, intimate, dynamic relationship.

Many couples have mastered *The Blueprint For Conscious Partnership* through working with me directly. They have shared that facing their inner demons and learning to embody the six qualities has them making love like never before, knowing how to turn up the erotic heat and share a passion that is deeper and more dynamic than it ever was in the early years of their relationship.

I am so glad you are here! I am glad you are open to another way of relating! You have suffered long enough, and now it's time to take your beautiful capacity for intellectual analysis, openhearted awareness, intuition, and erotic responsiveness, and learn how to use them in practical ways that will transform your relationship from the inside out.

Exercise

Before diving into *The Blueprint For Conscious Partnership*, take some time to identify your current beliefs about relationships. Sit down with pen and paper and journal on the following questions:

1. Are there particular beliefs you were exposed to in your family about what it means to be a good wife or husband?

2. How do you feel about those beliefs? Are they true for you? Are they in alignment with how you want to live?

3. Do you believe you have to sacrifice who you are for your relationship to last?

4. Do you believe your relationship supports you in being the best version of yourself?

5. Do you believe it's inevitable for passion to diminish with time?

6. Do you feel hopeful, scared, or otherwise about the future of your relationship, *regardless of how it is now*?

7. How are your beliefs influencing your current relationship with your partner?

CHAPTER 4

Celebrate Your Love

You may have found that when you are dissatisfied with your relationship, or rather with your partner, it's hard to look at him and think of anything else but your dissatisfaction. There are, of course, those moments that remind you what is special about him and how much you love him. But, for the most part, when couples are in a rut, each of them is more focused on what *isn't* working than what *is,* which in turn amplifies and colors every interaction.

When our needs aren't met, we typically feel activated or triggered, which results in us implementing one of the following coping mechanisms: *fight, flight, freeze or faint.* In childhood, when our needs aren't met, one of those responses becomes our main coping strategy. Thereafter, even when our needs are relatively well attended to and we aren't in any real danger, we still default to that kind of response when something feels unsatisfactory. This can play out in obvious ways and also in very subtle ways, as it is largely an unconscious process.

Maybe when your partner says something mildly hurtful to you, you "freeze" inside, which shows up with you inwardly feeling numb and ignoring it. Maybe when your partner does something and you don't like it, you respond by being nasty toward him, or your kids, or the Starbucks barista, or whomever you happen to be interacting with, because "fight" is your go to response. Maybe when things are uncomfortable between the two of you, your partner disappears. He might literally disappear and exit the room, or he might be physically present but internally absent. Either way he's gone, because "flight" is his go-to mode.

It's important to recognize the patterns in your relationship, both your own patterns and those of your partner's. In fact, one of the gifts of intimate relating is having a context to be able to see what your patterns actually are so you can transform them if you so desire. But before getting into dysfunctional patterns of relating and how to resolve them, it's absolutely imperative to remember *why* you are together in the first place.

When couples are in a challenging phase, on a down swing that is significant and painful, they are usually focused on what *isn't* working. While coaching a couple in such a phase, I might ask one of them what's going on. Often, the response is a litany of examples demonstrating a partner's shortcomings, hurtful actions, and all the ways the person sharing has been negatively impacted. When a couple is experiencing this kind of rough time, there may well be some lovely moments happening too, but the couple hardly notices.

I remember my father used to tell his experience of the dramatic arrival of strollers in New York City. Prior to my birth, he had lived there as an adult for eleven years and walked the streets of Manhattan many times every day, all over the city. Not once during that time had he ever noticed a stroller. After I was born, he was shocked to see them everywhere! Suddenly he encountered them on every street he walked, no matter where he was going. Likewise, when you are in a hard phase in your relationship, when you feel resentment and disappointment, when your feelings are hurt and your needs unmet, or you are just generally shut down and avoidant, you will look at your partner and only see a person who is the source of your feelings of disappointment and suffering. In that regard, your awareness is exactly like my father's before I was born and he began perceiving strollers in his environment. You are missing everything else that is there!

If you start working on your relationship and only see what *isn't* working, it's akin to building a structure on quicksand. To begin to build a stronger foundation, I advise my clients (especially in our first sessions) to spend some time identifying what drew them to one another in the first place. I ask her what she loves about him. I ask him when he knew that she was the one for him. I elicit the ways he has grown and hear her admiration for his choices. She may name his steadfastness or willingness to try new things. Of course, with each couple it's different but invariably they both share things they have never before spoken aloud.

It is immediately healing and opens hearts to hear such sentiments, to feel seen, admired, and appreciated. It's surprising both because she has never said it before, and because he has mostly heard her criticism and disappointment, the ways he has failed her, not what she loves.

Afterward, I turn to him and ask him to share what he loves about her, what drew him to her, and what keeps him there. And out comes a collection of heartfelt, tender, sometimes awkward expressions of the deepest love. I welcome his soulful gratitude for how she runs their household, and the way she giggles at dumb jokes. He names her beauty as well as her power.

Her worries that they aren't having sex because he is no longer attracted to her fall away, and she can feel his yearning and his respect, and often his awe of the woman she is. She has had no idea how much gratitude he feels for her, and how grateful he is for their partnership.

It's surprising how often women in committed couples doubt the devotion of their husband's, but in my experience, the devotion really is always there, under the surface, usually unspoken and unnamed, because to him it's so obvious. (And plus, she never asked!)

These moments are sacred, and definitive. Each couple that takes the time to do this, *especially* during rocky times when it is not intuitive to share the love so vulnerably, are forever changed. Their troubles aren't gone, but they finally are in proper perspective. Most of all they both connect with the mutual commitment they have to the relationship, to both their own and each other's wellbeing. The shared history and maturity of the relationship, and the consequent depth of connection, is palpable and they both feel it.

Evoking the love and beauty, and the couple's mutual respect for one another provides the context for all the work and transformation that follows. It's a magnificent step that feels akin to looking at a map together before heading out on a voyage.

Elana and Steve were in just such a situation: They had been married for nineteen years and, from the beginning neither felt completely understood or supported by the other. While they remained committed, they definitely had their ups and downs. Twice they had sought support from a therapist, first at five and then at eight years in. It had been helpful to get unstuck and shed the feeling of being in a crisis each time, but fundamentally everything stayed the same. Naturally, they had become skeptical about whether anyone would be able to help them.

I listened carefully to all of their challenges. They loved one another and were clearly committed to staying together. Also, they hadn't had sex in eight months. They never discussed anything but finances, kids and what the kids needed. And almost every evening they went their separate ways because it was too painful for her to initiate lovemaking only to be rejected. For him, it was unbearable to feel that he couldn't make her happy in bed so it was simpler to avoid it altogether. I listened to all of this with compassion, knowing that this had been their situation for many years.

Afterward, I asked them to share where they had met, what drew them together, and what they loved and appreciated about one another. As soon as they started recounting how they had met, sharing some of their stories about dating and getting engaged, the energy in the room instantly felt lighter. Their faces became more relaxed and the tone of their voices sounded more buoyant.

Elana talked about how much she admired Steve's willingness to try whatever new class or project she proposed, how handsome she found him, what a good father he was, and how much she appreciated that their values were aligned and they had the same priorities with money. As she spoke these things, she started glowing and warming up, letting herself feel the love. Steve in turn, relaxed his shoulders, and at one point, stoic as he was, wiped away a runaway tear.

When it was his time to speak, he took a moment to steady his voice, and then proceeded to share how proud he was to be with Elana. He named how beautiful and intelligent he found her, how she cared so lovingly for their home and for each member of their family, how she intuitively understood what they all needed and researched anything that might be helpful on their paths. He expressed that she was the love of his life and that being with her was his greatest happiness and proudest accomplishment.

Meanwhile, her demeanor changed dramatically, like a well-nourished chia pet coming to life, filling in all the dry places that had lead to her feeling depleted and taken for granted. She replaced

33

those feelings with hope, and a reinforced knowing that they were on the right path—together.

In that first session, sharing what they loved and appreciated about one another, Elana and Steve felt more love for each other than they had in a long while. They also felt the long-forgotten sensations of erotic heat. They felt better and more connected than they had in years. Their problems were exactly as they had been for months, but now they felt right-sized and held inside more love.

This kind of efficient, profound, life-altering shift is available to you too. Try it!

Exercise

- Take out a pen and paper.

- Write down what you love about your partner. Include what you love and admire about who he is in the world, what you appreciate about him as a human being, and what you are grateful for in terms of how he shows up for you and your family, and finally how he makes you feel.

- Resist adding qualifiers such as "when he's in a good mood" or "most of the time".

- Ask him to do the same for you.

- Arrange a time to be together when neither of you will be interrupted and share your discoveries with each other. You may use what you wrote as a guide for your conversation, read it verbatim, or a combination of the two. Do whatever feels right for you and allow your partner to do the same.

CHAPTER 5
Cultivate Curiosity

When you first fall in love, it is such an amazing feeling. And there is so much curiosity! You want to know everything about your partner. What is his favorite food? Does he like to travel? Does he like the mountains or the beach better? What was the name of his first grade teacher, and what was he like when he was six years old? What are his hopes and dreams for the future? What are some of his biggest fears? The questions are endless, and having them answered is one way you feel connected, intrigued, and beautifully bonded to your beloved. Typically, you just can't get enough of who they are and what matters to them.

And then, life happens, other things claim your attention. You have responsibilities at work and at home, plus now you know one another *really* well, so everything is no longer new and waiting to be discovered. Gradually (and sometimes rapidly) your attention shifts to other things, and the curiosity and drive to question and know who this person is falls away. In its place is routine and familiarity.

The safety and stability that comes with familiarity is undeniably wonderful to feel. But, in the process of creating that, something very important is lost. One consequence is that we start making assumptions about our partner. No longer asking questions, because we think we know the answers. And in many respects, we *do* know.

We know a lot. We know if our partner likes tea or coffee, what kinds of movies he prefers, favorite restaurants, and all kinds of other things too. Even so, there is *always* more to know and learn about your partner. We are all changing, evolving beings and it is essential to leave room for ongoing curiosity.

Do you know when your partner first had an experience of success? Do you know your partner's all time favorite birthday celebration? Do you know what he is daydreaming about these days? Do you know when your partner last told a white lie? Do you know what he found to be the most satisfying aspect of the past week? Or what music or program he is listening to while commuting to work? There are countless questions to ask when you feel curious and want to get to know your partner more deeply and when you are open to finding the elements of his personality and passions you haven't yet explored.

It's worth reiterating something from chapter one: The average couple in the US speaks about something other than kids and logistics with their significant other, for an average of less than four minutes a day. I found this hard to believe when I first heard it fifteen years ago because that is a lot of unshared dreams, frustrations, vulnerable truths, and spontaneous laughter. Years later, after coaching hundreds of couples, I absolutely believe the statistic is true.

If you want to increase the amount of time you and your partner are discussing other things, the best way to accomplish that is by making a point of asking your partner open-ended questions.

Open ended questions contrast with closed questions. Closed questions imply a finite number of possible responses. They receive answers of either yes or no or a choice between two or more options. Some examples are:

- Do you want to eat at home or go to the Chinese place around the corner?

- Do you want to invite your parents for Thanksgiving?

- Can you walk the dog when you get home?

In contrast, open ended questions don't require a single, particular response but rather, can lead anywhere. Some examples are:

- What are you excited about these days?

- Is there anything you'd like to discuss right now?

- Where do you see us in five years?

- What are your highest values?

- What are you worried about?

Such questions are invitations into our partner's soul. If you aren't used to asking such questions, it can feel awkward in the beginning, and also rather vulnerable. It can also be awkward to be asked such questions, therefore you may find that you ask an open-ended question and your partner responds as though it's a closed question or by brushing it off. Don't give up! You are both familiar with interacting in an entrenched way and it takes time and patience to create a new culture in your relationship; a culture of curiosity, spontaneity, and depth.

Once I explain this to couples, it's often fairly easy to begin to slow down, turn away from familiar exchanges, and start asking open-ended questions. The transition may run even more smoothly than expected because it feels good to make space for your partner to share. What is far less obvious, and sometimes challenging, is realizing it's key to respond to what was shared in a loving and encouraging way.

For example, if you ask your partner if he has a sexual fantasy he's never shared, and he courageously tells you what it is, it's essential that you don't respond by immediately shutting it down and indicating there's no way you are ever going to do that with him. Or perhaps you ask if there are any countries he would like to live in, and he shares he has always wanted to live in Nicaragua, and the first thing out of your mouth is that you are never going to live in Latin America.

The problem with responding in these ways is that your partner will internalize that it's dangerous to open up and share with you. It will confirm that it's not safe to share with you, because when he is vulnerable and honest, you respond with tension and criticism. This does not mean that you need to be a "yes" to whatever your partner shares. You just need to be a "yes" to the fact that he *is* sharing.

You might say, "I am so glad you shared that with me. I love knowing what you want." You could just leave it at that, or you might continue and say, "I didn't know you wanted to do that. It's not something that has ever attracted me, but I love knowing it turns you on." Over time, with practice, you will find your way with affirming whatever your partner happens to share, regardless of your feelings or thoughts about the content.

Women often find this distinction quite freeing. They want to be open-hearted and positive, and yet they also don't want to feel stuck between having a partner who doesn't share his truth or suppressing their own responses. Acknowledging and "being a yes" to the share provides the feeling of connection that both of you want, and it is understood that the content can be worked through independently. The key is to become someone with whom it's safe to share vulnerably, because without that feeling of safety, emotional intimacy and really passionate lovemaking will not be possible.

When I give talks, present at conferences, or am interviewed on podcasts, and I only have enough time to teach one tool, invariably the one I teach is: "Cultivate Curiosity". As a result, I have received some amazing testimonials from people whose only learning with me was to shift into asking open ended questions.

For example, my friend Rhonda is a wonderful personal trainer and she asked me to present a workshop at her gym. My presentation was entitled "How your Health Impacts Your Relationships and How Your Relationships Impact Your Health". Toward the end of the class, I taught about the importance of cultivating curiosity as an excellent next step to deepening relationship and creating connection.

Rhonda was fascinated by what I shared and said she would implement it right away. She was super busy and her husband worked very long hours as well. She was convinced that they didn't have fifteen minutes a day to connect about matters other than kids and logistics, at least not while she was alert and awake. I recommended they talk on the phone while he was commuting to work, with deliberate intention to avoid talking about kids and logistics and be open to what arose. The next morning he dropped the kids off at school and then drove to work. She was at home and made a point of being available to speak with him while he drove. She said:

> "When I presented the idea to Landon, the key component that had him willing to participate, was hearing that we would both be a full yes to one another, not in regard to the content, but with regard to being open to the ideas we would share: No judgment, No problem solving. Just honoring one

another for the willingness to share meaningfully. I also named how awkward it was because we are not in the habit of talking in this way. Basically, I set it up so the awkwardness would be expected and even become a part of our conversation, rather than a reason to avoid it. I started our conversation with a question on a topic that I know he loves, even though I don't love it, namely his motorcycle. It's been a contentious topic for us, but I really was open and curious and asked him what he loves about it, and what his experience is when he rides it. He told me what the bike means to him and how he feels when he rides it. Because I was open, I could really see how great it is for him to have the bike, how it provides beautiful opportunities that serve and support him. It was really sweet and this complicated topic ended up bringing us closer together. It was so fun and beautiful. At the end, we both said that we felt good and more connected than we had felt in a long time. Also, there was a ripple effect from that one conversation in that there has been more softness and connection and subtle shifts that feel new and hopeful. I'm amazed that it just took me putting attention on having an open ended conversation and being curious!"

Curiosity will also serve you well during times of conflict. When you and your partner are butting heads as a result of not seeing eye to eye, whether it's something extremely important or not, one of the best ways to change the dynamic, and get out of polarized positioning, is to stop, take a breath, and ask an open-ended question. Keep in mind that this is not the time to ask a question intended to prove your point and show your partner exactly how wrong he is. That would be masking self-righteousness with curiosity. The purpose of disrupting the communication with an open ended question is that his answer will help you see his point of view. You may even find you see some truth in his perspective. As soon as you make that shift, you promptly change the shared dynamic from one that is win-lose to one that is win-win. With genuine curiosity, you are actually exploring how he might see things, rather than being set on proving him wrong.

I suggest that the next time you have an argument with your partner, or a difference of opinion with anyone for that matter, be curious and see what happens!

We all yearn to feel seen and heard, most especially by our romantic partners. In even the toughest of circumstances, curiosity paves the way. Where being locked in a right-wrong dynamic leads to disconnection, curiosity naturally creates and enhances connection.

Exercise

- Make a list of open-ended questions to ask your partner. (Refer back to some examples and make up your own.)

- Plan a time to be together without distractions and ask your partner the questions on your list. Make a point of listening with an open heart.

- Appreciate that your partner *is* sharing with you regardless of how you feel *about* the specific content shared.

CHAPTER 6
Vulnerability Matters

Learning how to share what is important for you, with your beloved, is essential to a fantastic relationship. You may have been raised with the teaching, "If you don't have anything nice to say, don't say anything at all." There are indeed many situations in which that is wise counsel, and our world certainly could use a little more civility and embodiment of that attitude. It is particularly apt when speaking with children, when navigating office politics, and when chatting with neighbors. However, in intimate relating, that approach can be damaging. Because if you are withholding something that matters to you, it creates a disruption in your connection. It's as if an invisible wall is formed between you and your partner and it's constructed from the material of the important things you are not saying.

When you share your life with someone, and you withhold important truths, it becomes impossible to have unfettered openhearted connection. In fact, when I first became a coach, I learned something that surprised me until I understood it better. Couples would approach me, tentatively, because their sex life was infrequent and unsatisfying. Even though each of them felt sad, rejected, powerless, and perhaps numb, they didn't want to express anything unpleasant about their partner. Their priority was being respectful towards one another, and honoring their relationship. In such situations my first focus was guiding the couple to have more rapport and ease while sharing honestly and vulnerably.

In the context of marriage and long term committed relationships, emotional connection is essential for great sex. So I would begin our work together by helping couples in this situation create a culture of honesty, vulnerability, and courageous sharing. I anticipated, once they were honest with one another and able to share authentically, that we would then shift focus to more explicitly address sexuality, bedroom techniques, and how to touch one another for maximum delight and expansive pleasure.

In the early days of my career, I thought I needed to begin with teaching couples how to embrace honesty, sharing the communication tools described in this chapter. Meanwhile I planned to segue into talking about sex a few sessions later. However, I found when the couple was being honest with themselves and one another, and it was time to shift into talking about sex and what was happening in their bedroom, invariably, the couple would light up, giggle, and assure me that was no longer necessary. In other words, where I thought I needed to teach communication and then focus on sex, in fact I just needed to teach couples how to be emotionally present and vulnerable. Eight out of every ten couples would translate that emotional intimacy right into sensual and sexual connection.

Jenny and David hadn't had sex in nine months. In an early session, I had them share what they love about one another and then taught them the importance of expressing their truth to one another. I also taught them exactly how to do so, with a schema that is incredibly easy to follow. Since learning how to communicate with depth and vulnerability, and doing so regularly, they have been having nourishing sex consistently and feeling extremely happy with their sensual experiences. They are so relieved!

I have found that when couples learn how to be honest, vulnerable, and curious, along with cultivating the other qualities detailed in this book, the most common outcome is fulfilling, passionate sex. In fact, the sex is typically better than it was when the relationship was new.

So, you are probably wondering, how exactly does this work? Well, I want to begin by distinguishing between *brutal* honesty and *vulnerable* honesty:

Brutal Honesty

Every now and then someone hears me speak about the importance of embracing honesty and confuses that with turning to their partner and telling them everything, everything they can think of that they haven't said before. This happens while paying little attention to the impact of either the content or tone. On the receiving end, this usually feels terrible, cruel, and shocking. Ultimately, the sharer ends up feeling remorseful and comes to the conclusion that honesty and sharing are not wise ideas.

With brutal honesty, you are focused on your own experience. You speak without regard for how it will be for your partner to hear what you are saying. This is fundamentally no better than being so focused on your partner's comfort, and not wanting to upset him, that you therefore avoid saying a lot of things you know to be true but are keeping to yourself. Withholding (for the sake of your partner's comfort) and brutal honesty (where you disregard your partner's experience) are two extremes and neither one of them fosters connection.

Vulnerable Honesty

With vulnerable honesty, you definitely have your attention on your own experience. You honor it and experience the sovereignty that comes from knowing that all of your insights, awareness, understanding, perspective, and most of all your *desires* are important, even essential, to the health of your relationship. You also are oriented toward your partner and his experience while he hears what you share. Both holding back and sharing without care lead to disconnection. The middle ground, vulnerable sharing, is the secret sauce to happiness and feeling whole. It is the bedrock of lasting passion.

Why do people withhold?

There are three distinct reasons, and you have probably experienced all three of them in one circumstance or another. The first reason you might withhold from your partner is that you don't actually *know* what you want. This is not about lacking the words to say it to your partner – this is about not having the words to say it to yourself!

This scenario is common if you are a nurturer and tend to martyr yourself, ignoring your own needs while making sure everyone else is happy. This is also a likely scenario if you are a high achiever, focused on what to do next in order to achieve your goals, never having put much attention on *being*. You probably always know what your next goals are, but do not know your current desires. This can be simplified by saying you know what you *should* do but not necessarily what you *want* to do.

Even though you might be perfectly clear about what you want in your career, if you are not sure what you want in your relationship, it is key to learn how to allow your desires to come into your consciousness, so you can befriend them and let them guide you. If that is something you struggle with, this action guide will be quite useful. https://alexandrastockwell.com/desire

The second reason you might withhold important truth from your partner is that you don't want to hurt him. In healthy relationships, including toleration relationships, we do not want to hurt our partners. If you carry a truth that you know will be painful for your partner to hear, that in itself can feel like reason enough not to say it. One of the things that is often the most difficult for a couple to accept is the inevitability that they will cause one another pain. It is part and parcel of deep love. Learning to share something important, even when it will be hard for your partner to hear, is an essential skill in conscious partnership.

The third reason you might withhold from your partner is not wanting to deal with your partner's response. If you know that sharing your truth will cause your partner to become extremely angry or sad, it takes extra courage to share. Anticipating the unpleasant intensity afterwards becomes an impediment as dealing with the fallout is a real deterrent to sharing.

From my perspective, the question is never whether or not to share. It is *how* to share.

If you are not in the habit of sharing vulnerably, it can feel tentative and intimidating to do so. You might be quite comfortable being critical, which is akin to brutal honesty. You might frequently opt not to say anything, becoming resentful instead. Regardless of your way of handling this in the past, gently and vulnerably sharing your thoughts and feelings is essential and it takes courage!

You may read this chapter to this point and be inspired to see what happens when you share something vulnerable with your partner. You may start out softly, trying it out to see how it goes, like sending the proverbial canary into the coal mine. However, if you are being ever so subtle in order to assess your partner's response, it's likely that your partner won't notice anything at all. Even though you lean in and take the risk, chances are it will be too discrete for him to notice. Therefore he won't respond in a way that feels affirming for you, which can be very frustrating, especially since you have gone out on a limb.

You might then conclude that being vulnerable doesn't work, that in fact it's worse because you just feel even more unseen and frustrated than before. But you would be incorrect in coming to that conclusion. It's true, he might not care about what you are saying, but then again he might. Either way, you have not set things up in a way that yields valuable data. You don't yet have enough information to determine whether or not the tool will bear fruit.

Let me guide you a bit: It's important to start the conversation by saying that you have something vulnerable to share, and asking if he's available to hear it. Here are a few examples of ways to transition into a vulnerable share, that will set you up for greater success:

- I have something vulnerable to share with you. Are you available to hear it now?

- I have something that is complicated for me that I want to share with you. Is this a good time?

- There is something I want to share with you, but it's uncomfortable for me to say it and I will need your full attention in order to do so. Are you open to hearing it now?

When you ask questions like these, even if it feels hard to do, it is imperative that you are open to hearing "yes" or "no" as equally acceptable answers. Obviously, you would like the answer to be yes.

But if it's no, you need to accept it without making a big deal about it. Please understand, if it's not a good moment for him to hear it, it is definitely not going to go well for you to share something tender or complex.

If the two of you are devoted to having a great relationship, then "no" is more helpfully seen as a "not yet." When my husband has had a long day caring for patients and comes home for dinner, I might say to him that I have something vulnerable to share and ask if he's available to hear it. He might respond with "I am not, but after I have some dinner and take a shower, I will be ready and glad to listen." Or I might be preoccupied with something work-related and not able to be fully present in the way such a moment asks for, so I would answer "Yes, I want to hear it, but I need a few moments to clear my head. I will be available in ten minutes." And then it would be my job to throw cold water on my face or meditate or do something concrete to shift my energy.

Once your partner says yes, to being available, the next thing to share is *why* you are telling him. This step is very important and only comes after you figure that out for yourself. It requires you to do some self-inquiry and be aware of *why* it's important. Some possible reasons might be:

- It's been bothering me, and I really want to clear the air between us.

- Every time I look at you, I think about this thing and it results in me feeling disconnected from you.

- It's really important to me and I need you to know it too.

After sharing why you are making this communication, the third and final step before making the communication is to share your desired outcome. The desired outcome is what will make the share a win-win for both of you and for your relationship.

I learned the importance of the third step once I realized *how* my husband listened to me on a regular basis. Before I knew to communicate this way, if I would start sharing something vulnerable, especially if it was about my husband or our relationship or our sex life or anything that involved him, he would be listening, just waiting for me to tell him what he was doing wrong. He braced himself to hear how he had messed up, how he hadn't done a good enough job, or something of that sort. Either way, he was listening while feeling like he would never be good enough.

I have told him exactly how inadequate his actions were, many times over, in the context of blaming him for the quality of my experience. But many other times, I wasn't telling him he had done something wrong. Instead I just wanted him to know what was happening inside me so we could be more connected. Because I have been critical in the past, often, and also because he had a proclivity to feel he wasn't good enough to begin with, as soon as I began to speak, that was often where his mind would go. So, rather than being relaxed and present, oriented to co-creating a win-win situation, he would brace himself for the negativity and accusations he was certain would be hurled upon him.

Once I learned to share my desired outcome, and make sure it was a win-win that would appeal to *both* of us, he was able to be present, listen more deeply, and be far more open to what I was actually saying.

Examples of win-win outcomes include:

- My desired outcome in sharing this with you is that we can really understand one another's point of view and feel happy and connected again.

- My desired outcome is that I share with you and feel heard, and you know where I am coming from, so that from there we can identify a solution that works for both of us.

- My desired outcome is that I won't be holding onto this resentment anymore and then, we can transition into a sexy evening in the bedroom together.

My clients Sharla and Tim use this way of communicating on a regular basis. Recently, she woke up early before going to the gym, and saw that there were dishes in the sink even though Tim had said he would do them. Later that evening Sharla said to Tim, "I have something vulnerable to share with you. Are you available to hear it now?"

Tim is a physician, and he had a few emails to send before being completely done with his workday. He said, "I just need to send a few emails and then I will be available."

So, fifteen minutes later, they sat down together on their blue velvet couch, and Sharla said, "I want to share this with you because it is really important to me and it's been eating at me all day. My desired outcome in sharing it with you is that you will know my experience and then we will both feel more connected and be ready to transition to the bedroom, both fully present and undistracted."

Tim responded, "That sounds good."

Sharla then said, "I really appreciate your willingness to do the dishes last night. I had a lot going on and it was helpful when you said you would do them. When I woke up this morning and found last night's dinner dishes in the sink, my heart sank. It's not just that the dishes weren't done, it's that I feel taken for granted, that my experience doesn't matter, that you don't love me enough to do something which makes a huge difference for me. It's not just about doing the dishes, it's about me feeling unsupported and like I have to do everything myself or it won't get done. I feel myself pulling back and becoming resentful. And I feel scared too, because I don't feel attracted to you when I am in this state."

Tim responded, "Thank you so much for telling me. I didn't know it would be that way for you. I was tired and thought I would just do them this morning, and I didn't mean to communicate any of that to you."

"Thank you."

And they didn't need to discuss it further. No processing necessary, because vulnerable honesty often shifts *everything*. Flirtatious body language followed, and Sharla and Tim felt closer.

Julee used this way of communicating after she found out that her husband Sam had put a down payment on a cabin about two hours from where they lived:

"I have something intense and vulnerable to share with you. Are you available to hear it?"

"Yes," Sam said.

"Thank you. I want to share it with you because I have a lot of feelings and if I don't, and I keep it in, it is going to fester and rot inside my soul and will definitely impact our relationship and I don't want that to happen. My desired outcome is that we can connect with one other more deeply and figure out how to be more collaborative and have everything feel really good between us."

"Sounds good. Go ahead."

"I know that you were excited about the cabin, and that you showed me the pictures last week. But I had no idea you were so close to putting a deposit down on it. I actually like it and I am excited to have a weekend getaway. We have both been wanting that since forever, but I am really hurt, confused, and kind of shocked, that you went ahead and paid the deposit without even discussing it with me. You mentioning it and my not stating any objections is definitely not the same as discussing it with me. If you had discussed it, we probably would have ended up going ahead with it anyway, but if you don't discuss that with me, I feel unimportant, ancillary, and like you don't see my value here. This is a relationship where I want to make all important decisions collaboratively. Yes, you are the real estate investor and you recognize good deals, but we are married, and this is going to make a big difference in how we spend our time together, especially on the weekends, and it is really important to me to be a part of this decision."

Sam felt stunned. He thought they had discussed it. But he knew the goal was to be more collaborative so rather than responding with a defensive position and argumentative tone to counter what she said, he paused and took a breath. Then, he asked a few open-ended questions. He also clarified her understanding of the conversations they had had, since he thought those exchanges had been the two of them discussing it, and obviously she did not feel this way at all.

When sharing your truth, there are two elements to consider: First, the communication tool and second, the specific content. It is really important to practice using the tool. Namely, to begin by asking your partner if he's available. If he is, say why you want to make the share, and what your desired outcome is. This is not an invitation to share so you can blame your partner or point out what a jerk he was. It is vulnerable sharing, which means you are revealing your experience, the impact something has had on you, and/or the story you are telling yourself. Through sharing the truth for you, the tender reality that your partner can only access if you choose to reveal it, you will discover the communication channel between you opens. Once that happens, all kinds of energies can begin to flow.

Exercise

- Make a list of things you haven't shared with your partner. Include smaller, more mundane things like saying you liked last night's movie because he liked it so much when actually you found it boring. Or how you feel taken for granted when he doesn't help with cooking or cleaning.

- Also include bigger things, like the fact that you usually fake your orgasms, or you felt unsupported by his presence when you gave birth six years ago and you still haven't forgiven him for that, or that you had a one night stand while on a business trip eight years ago, or that you saw the flirtatious texts on his phone from his secretary and just ignored them but have been less passionate with him ever since because you feel betrayed.

- Write down whatever comes to mind, without judging it. The list is for you to be clear on how much and what kinds of things you are withholding.

- Next, find the most benign thing on your list and use the three-part way of sharing to talk to your partner about that particular item. If and when that goes well, pick something a little edgier, but still relatively benign.

- You both need to learn to communicate in this way, sharing vulnerably and focused on win/win outcomes. Practicing communicating in this way will build your confidence and your skill. In the process you will become prepared to share more confronting, vulnerable truths and to experience the freedom and connection that comes from sharing in service of improving your relationship.

CHAPTER 7

Kindness Is the Key to Successful Communication

Let's distinguish between being nice and being kind. In building intimacy, being *kind is* essential while being *nice* is often stifling.

When you are nice, you are typically (whether you are aware of it or not) thinking of the other person's feelings, adjusting what you say and how you say it to make the other person more comfortable. This means if your husband doesn't like loud noises you don't raise your voice. If your husband might feel hurt, you don't tell him that you don't like the earrings he just gave you. It means *not s*haring that you didn't enjoy being touched the way he touched you last night, because it may be a blow to his ego.

I am certainly not advocating the opposite, namely focusing on your experience and feelings without regard to your partner's. Instead, I invite you to consider the middle ground between putting your partner's comfort level above all else and expressing your unfiltered inner process.

In reality, the enlightened middle ground is where real kindness resides.

When you are kind, you have your attention on your own inner experience, needs and desires, and you also have attention on your partner's experience and how you are impacting him. When you are either being nice or being selfish you create disconnection, because you aren't honoring both of you in your communication, and being kind is fundamentally relational. Being kind also allows you to communicate with love and care. What would otherwise be hard to hear, when communicated with kindness, is much easier for whomever you are speaking to, to take in and consider.

Being kind is a concept that is fairly easy to understand but implementing it is one of the most challenging aspects of a relationship. One of the primary ways we become kind, is by adjusting the *tone* we use when we speak.

Very often we are unaware of our tone and therefore don't realize its impact. If you say something to your partner and he becomes defensive and you wonder why, evaluate your tone. Tone of voice is often how both intended and unintended feelings of criticism, dismissal, judgment and resentment seep through, and if your partner is responding as though you are being unkind it is highly likely that your tone reflects that.

When I began coaching couples, I had the privilege of experiencing them speaking with one another in ways that were not witnessed by others. Again and again, I was somewhat shocked by how women in good, strong relationships spoke with their partners, subtly or overtly putting them down in direct communications. I also saw this in how she spoke to me about her partner, in the third person, while the three of us were in conversation in the same room together. I heard statements like:

- I'm so over how careless he is with money. It's like he's trying to make sure our kids won't go to college.

- I'm so sick of him wearing that ugly sweatshirt. Can't you figure out how to just buy something online?

- Everyday, it's the same thing with him. I'm so bored, I practically want to fall asleep."

When I first witnessed this behavior I was really surprised and then I realized it was exactly how I sometimes spoke with my husband. Without observing others, I never would have recognized that my tone of voice was unkind; it seemed normal and not the least bit noteworthy. In fact, if my husband had requested I speak more kindly to him I would have been certain I was already doing so.

Culturally, as empowered modern women, we are used to speaking to our male partners in ways we would never want to be spoken to ourselves. It's subtle and often easier to see our unpleasantness in hindsight rather than in present time. Pivoting into kindness is actually quite nuanced and often more easily appreciated *after* the change has been made.

In practice, embracing honesty and being kind are intertwined. They are conceptually distinct, but they really need to be implemented at the same time because embracing honesty focuses on the content conveyed and being kind focuses on the manner with which it is conveyed. Both are fundamentally necessary in order to improve communication.

Kindness is most often conveyed in our tone of voice. We can say the exact same words, but when we are unkind we can sound derisive, judgmental, dismissive, superior, skeptical, resentful, and angry. In contrast, when we are being kind, our tone can be soft, warm, humble, direct, uncomplicated, and loving. In fact, thirty percent of what we communicate is conveyed through the tone of our voices and it's invariably the portion we are least aware of.

Most of the time, when a couple has a difference of opinion it creates a recurring dynamic: Whether it is an outright disagreement or just inferred. and whether the conflict is blatant or more controlled, dramatic or subtle, invariably the issue is eventually put aside. You both recognize that you don't know how to move through it, and since you can't figure out how to create a new resolution that works for everyone, you let it go. However, despite your best intentions to avoid the trap of an altogether familiar and painful dynamic, it eventually arises anyway. You try to avoid it but even so, every now and then, it's back and sure enough you both have the same emotional and intellectual positions. It feels achingly familiar and so excruciatingly mired.

Alternatively, you may be the kind of couple that processes things, talking everything through over and over. This means that once the emotional intensity of the conflict has blown over, you discuss it. You hear his side of things and you share yours. Hours (sometimes days) later, you come to a new understanding and appreciation of one another's positions, anticipating things will feel more collaborative going forward and then, as if you had never thoroughly worked it through, you find yourself in an almost identical dynamic the next time the issue arises. Maybe it's a little simpler the next time because you know where your partner is coming from, and maybe it's a little worse because you both know where the other is coming from and can use that against each other. Either way, processing is helpful in mitigating things *after* the fact and getting to know one another better, but it doesn't actually *prevent* the conflict from recurring.

The problem with processing is that understanding is rarely enough to create new behavior. This is why you have probably experienced having a conflict, processing it, only to find yourself in the same conflict again, feeling as though you never worked it through previously. This cycle is frustrating and sometimes paves the way back to the first scenario, where you just let the issue go because talking about it ultimately feels futile and it's too frustrating to feel that way.

Happily, there is an excellent way to break this cycle; there is another alternative besides avoidance and analysis. Instead, you can create new experiences that are wholesome and harmonious, innovative and honest, by doing what I describe as *a conscious redo*. The conscious redo is designed to form new ways of feeling, communicating, and acting mid-conflict; you can access new experiences and never have to go back and relive the exact same frustrations again. The dictionary definition of redo is "to do something again, especially in order to do it better." The potency of this tool comes from using it repeatedly. Each time you use it, you will become more skillful with it, eventually learning to employ it right in the middle of the conflict, while you are literally in the heat of the moment.

Instead of processing and understanding, and having a deja vu experience as you start the conflict all over again, you stop and *redo* your communications in the moment. You make a conscious choice to create a new experience that is more satisfying for both of you. From a neurological perspective, it means that you create new neural pathways in response to the same trigger, instead of firing the same pathways again and again. This results in the formation of new habits while in the midst of intense emotions. The result is freedom from the compulsion of the familiar dynamic, and the creativity to interact more productively.

A successful conscious redo requires a lot of awareness in both of you, as well as courage and the willingness to be vulnerable. It takes practice to become aware while feeling activated, to internally create enough space to take a short time out, regroup, and then proceed in a new and improved, much kinder way. This is a learnable skill and with practice comes the ability to participate in successful conscious redos.

When you have the desire to apologize for what you said or how you said it, when you find yourself in a familiar dynamic that you don't enjoy, when you feel insulted, attacked, or otherwise disrespected by your partner, these are all moments to disrupt the dynamic. Pause for a moment and request a conscious redo.

Either one of you can request the conscious redo, whether you want to redo how you have spoken, or you want to redo how you were spoken to. Initially it is common for the person who is spoken to in an unkind way to recognize that a redo is necessary. With practice, you may find yourself becoming much more conscious of both how you feel and how you speak. When you don't like how you feel or sound, you can request a conscious redo because you want to practice showing up more lovingly in your relationship and you want both you and your partner to feel that painful interactions can be alchemized.

It really doesn't matter who makes the request. Either way, the one who didn't make the request always has full permission to say yes, no, or not yet. If the requested partner isn't ready, wait until a better time and then proceed with the conscious redo, starting from just before the communications became problematic. If a person doesn't want to do a conscious redo, it is often because the person is so angry or otherwise distraught that they can't access another way of communicating in that moment. In this case, it is best to take a true intermission in the conversation and wait to return to it once both people can be present, non-reactive, and are able to choose how they behave.

Sometimes one partner requests a conscious redo, and the other partner doesn't know what to adjust because it felt fine the first time. In that scenario, the partner who requested the conscious redo should state as simply as possible what was unpleasant for them. It is important to describe your own experience rather than blaming your partner for doing something wrong.

Definitely *do* say: I would like a conscious redo because I felt very uncomfortable when you said that.

Definitely do *not* say, I would like a conscious redo because you attacked me.

Requesting a conscious redo is not intended as a means to make your partner feel bad, to get him to apologize to you, or to pressure him into admitting any wrongdoing. The real power in this exercise comes with growing your ability to access self-awareness, and courage, in order to take control of your own emotions and tone, and then shift them.

In learning to shift, it is important to remember that the point is not to shrink or minimize your experience; it is for you to learn to express it more effectively. A conscious redo also is not a method for controlling your partner, and having him speak exactly as you prescribe. It is used for the development of internal agility, the capacity to pivot and then speak your truth with a fresh perspective. The conscious redo provides a context to affirm that what you say is important, and how it feels to your partner to hear it is also important.

When my clients start doing conscious redos, they find, that initially they are motivated by wanting to speak differently for their partner's sake. With practice, they become motivated by the power, freedom, and internal spaciousness which is the happy consequence of mastering one's own internal landscape; it constitutes access to the most effective ways to grow yourself, your relationship, and your depth of connection.

Being kind occurs through your tone, your facial expressions, and leaning in with loving interest and open-hearted curiosity. Kindness is also conveyed through the quality of your presence while you communicate, which is always important and especially so during challenging and vulnerable conversations.

I have done some of my best learning when my husband requested a conscious redo and I didn't know why. In such a situation I would ask him to tell me what to adjust, because knowing what to shift is essential to doing it better the next time! The times I didn't know why he was requesting a conscious redo are when I have learned the most about how I impact others. I have also learned how to pivot so that the quality of my communication is exactly what I want it to be, and I never would have had the opportunity to learn that if Rodd didn't request conscious redos during the times I considered my communication to have been quite good and he did not.

Tyla and John were talking about packing their son's lunch. Tyla had a major deadline and was going to be leaving earlier than usual in the morning and had asked John to pack their seven-year-old son Jacob's lunch for the day. On her way out the door Tyla said to John, as he was putting mayonnaise on the bread, "Don't give him turkey." John said, "Fine, you make it then."

Tyla was shocked and angry. She felt undermined and was furious that this was happening on a morning when she needed to leave and had set everything up ahead of time to make it easier for her to get out the door. In the past she would have yelled at him, telling him what a jerk he was and how she could never count on him and this sucked. Then she would have slapped together some peanut butter and jelly for Jacob, and left later than planned. On her way to work she would have felt entitled to her "poor me" story, sulking about what she has to put up with in her marriage.

Tyla saw all that in an instant and instead, she stopped a moment, centered herself, and requested a conscious redo. John's shoulders were tight as he anticipated the barrage of frustration, anger, and criticism likely coming his way. When she requested the conscious redo he relaxed, and agreed to it. Tyla then turned, looked at him with her full attention and said in a clear, kind tone, "I really appreciate you making Jacob's lunch today. I should have discussed with you how to have this work best for all three of us. He doesn't like turkey sandwiches and I should have told you that. Would you please make him something else instead? At this point, peanut butter and jelly is probably the best choice." John smiled and said, "Sure. I am glad to know." And then, "I've got this. Go ahead to work so you aren't late."

Sometimes the conscious redo has more words as it did with Tyla and John. Other times it's actually fewer words and very simple, like this:

"Trevor, pick your shit up off the floor." Said with exasperation by Sally, as she is getting out of the shower and finds Trevor's clothes from yesterday in her way. Trevor doesn't respond, and instead he asks for a conscious redo. Sally agrees and says, "Please move your clothes from the floor" in a clear, uncomplicated, kind way. Trevor says, "Sure, sorry about that." He gets up and simply moves his clothes.

Conscious redos create joy in the form of second chances!

Exercise

- The next time one of you finds a communication unpleasant for any reason it's an opportunity to request a conscious redo. Before making the request, it is important to center yourself. Then make the request as lovingly and calmly as possible, doing it in a way that your partner will want to agree to. Note that either one of you can request the conscious redo; it applies whether you want to be spoken to differently, or you want to speak to your partner differently, or both! The request can be made when a communication is a little bit off or unpleasant and it can also come in the midst of a full-blown disagreement with a great deal of emotional charge. The technique is the same regardless of the intensity of the situation (though it is much easier to implement in relatively mild moments).

- When you request a conscious redo, take a moment to breathe and become present with yourselves. Only once both of you are ready, then proceed:

- Begin a conscious redo by repeating a moment that worked for both of you and move from that point into being loving, kind, vulnerable, honest, and connected as you say things differently. Be compassionate with yourselves if it takes a few tries to make such changes in how you communicate. It's not unusual when learning how to do conscious redos to need to attempt it multiple times. Your aim should be to improve incrementally with each redo. Just keep trying because it's a process! I promise, when you begin to experience improvements, it will feel empowering for both of you. This will increase feelings of mastery and intimacy. You'll begin to feel like no matter what transpires, there is always the opportunity for another (much better) try.

CHAPTER 8

Choosing Happiness

Have you heard the saying, "You can be right or you can be happy?"

That saying is a truth bomb and in my opinion, it's worth unpacking.

You might respond by saying "Why can't I be right *and* be happy? After all, being right often feels gratifying and triumphant and is therefore a feeling to aim for, isn't it?"

Well, yes, however, if you are in a relationship and you are focused on being right, what that usually means is that your partner needs to be wrong. For most people being right implies that other viewpoints, feelings, and experiences are wrong. Among people who accept the value of multiple points of view this need not be true. However, it's easier to grant other points of view in academic settings and business contexts than it is when making important decisions with a spouse or in the midst of conversations about painful subjects.

There are actually two distinct issues with being right: The first one is related to making your partner wrong. Being right can be gratifying in the short term, but ultimately it works against you, because being wrong is *not* sexy at all. If you think your partner is wrong on a regular basis, you are likely to find it difficult to be attracted to him. Who could be attracted to someone who is constantly wrong? Respect, admiration, and erotic heat are not readily available in a relationship where people are regularly and habitually finding each other wrong.

The other reason that being right undermines the health of your relationship is that it comes from a place of certainty, which is the opposite of being curious. Being right is a form of close-mindedness and creates barriers to real connection.

You might think the goal of a conflict is to win, but it isn't. The *real* goal of a conflict is to *understand* both yourself and your partner better. It allows you to see what matters to you, and it provides a context to reveal mismatches between your values and your experience.

One of the best illustrations of the importance of choosing to be happy rather than being right is in the Hindu legend known as *The Six Blind Men and The Elephant*. The story goes like this:

After hearing about elephants at length, six blind men finally have the opportunity to touch one. Each blind man reaches out and feels a different part of the elephant's body. The one who feels the elephant's leg says an elephant is like a pillar. The one who feels the elephant's tail says it's like a rope. The one who feels the elephant's ear says it's like a fan. The one who feels the elephant's massive side says it's like a wall. The one who feels the elephant's trunk says it's like a thick snake. The one who feels the elephant's tusk says it's like a spear. All six men have complete conviction that they are *right* based on their respective experiences. Indeed, each is correct in his evaluation and yet each of their experiences of the elephant are unique!

Choosing happiness is an essential quality of conscious partnership and yet this skill is sometimes misconstrued as acquiescence or suppressing the truth of how you really feel. This has been referred to as spiritual bypassing, where you opt for happiness without ever addressing the thing that wasn't working for you. That is definitely not what I am talking about here. Instead, it is the prioritization of curiosity, honesty and kindness by the people in the relationship. Built on such a foundation, choosing happiness leads to empowerment, freedom, and personal power. This power can be used to navigate any kind of wonderful or challenging situation.

Choosing happiness is an invitation to make an internal shift that you can access at any time. It is a simple choice that is always available and can be employed to improve any moment, requiring only personal agency and fortitude.

I first explored the skill of choosing happiness when I was a full-time mother, with three young children at home. I loved being a mother and I loved being at home, however, my patience and inner reserves were routinely worn out by the end of the day. Wanting my children to clean up their toys, while making and then serving dinner, were not my happiest times. My husband would come home and I appreciated the support, but still, I was stretched too thin and had a shorter fuse. I watched myself become resentful and I didn't like it.

After all, this was my life and I wanted to enjoy it! There was no one who was going to help me at home so I could take a few hours off on a regular basis to rejuvenate myself. We were not in a position to go on romantic dates as a way to bring more joy into my home and into my marriage. So instead, I needed to figure out how to make our everyday lives more erotically charged, I needed to figure out how to choose happiness.

I described earlier that I bought myself a French maid's apron to cook in and discarded all of my darker colored, practical ones. It sounds simple, but that one change brought a smile to my face, and showed me how small changes could lead to real happiness, and it was up to me to make them.

I enjoyed experimenting and bringing my creativity to the challenge. One day, as I cooked, I slowed my movements while sautéing vegetables. Another day, I did provocative hip circles as I washed dishes. I took the time to savor the smells filling my kitchen, and treated the pretty designs on my dishes inherited from my grandmother as art. I felt my apron moving back and forth along my body, in flow with my feminine movements. I naturally breathed more slowly and more deeply. My voice lowered and my heart opened.

One evening, I sat across from my husband at our dining table. Instead of looking at him as a co-parent here to help me herd our brood, I looked at him and made a point of seeing the handsome man he is. I let myself have the internal experience I might have if I saw him sitting at a bar. I felt my genitals soften and moisten, and I swayed my hips ever so slightly in my chair as I served pasta and chicken.

The most amazing aspect was to feel delight in the mundane. It was completely gratifying. I was never going to eliminate the mundane while raising young children so finding a way to really enjoy it was a premium discovery. On top of that, I noticed an immediate and positive impact on my whole family. My husband was more present and responded as a person does when feeling seen and received as a whole being. I had shifted from treating him as a co-parent to my sexy man who was collaborating with me in parenting our children.

With this change, my children were also more at ease. They listened more, they were more patient with one another, and quickly became altogether more enjoyable. Our dinner conversation was engaging and dynamic, and the mood consistently pleasant.

I never *said* anything to achieve this wonderful transformation. What I *did* was no more and no less than shifting where I put my attention, what my priorities were, and how I felt inside. I *chose* happiness and the results were magnificent.

If a French maid's apron is not your cup of tea, I urge you to find something that is. It should be something that lights you up and might even feel a little naughty: a feather boa perhaps, a sly looking hat, heels, or a bit of red glossy lipstick, playing sultry jazz at times of day that used to be challenging…the options are limitless.

A prerequisite to choosing happiness is clearing your resentments, and doing so on a regular basis. This guarantees that choosing happiness is not a form of spiritual bypass; you are not sidestepping your resentments because you are clearing them first.

There are many ways to clear resentments. It's best to commit to a method you resonate with and will also use consistently. Physical methods include vigorous exercise, yoga, or being in nature. Emotional methods include receiving bodywork or expressing how you feel to a trusted friend, therapist or coach. Another option is to write letters to whomever you resent (without sending them). Hypnotherapy, Byron Katie's "The Work" and similar modalities can also help. Meditation and prayer are spiritual ways. This list is not exhaustive, and no one way is better than another for clearing resentments. Anything that helps you release stuck feelings of anger, grief, resentment, sadness, feeling misunderstood or unimportant are excellent ways. Once you let such feelings go, you have the internal freedom and inner spaciousness to begin to choose happiness more often.

One of the most common pitfalls that couples face when they are in challenging times in their relationship is focusing on what isn't working. Typically, by the time a couple seeks professional guidance, they will be very focused on frustrations in the relationship and the ways their needs aren't being met. This often leads to forgetting what's actually wonderful about the relationship. The exercise at the end of chapter four invited you to look at what you love about your partner and the ways your relationship has already been serving you. Now it's time to identify some reliable ways for the two of you to enjoy yourselves while spending time together. The Fun Activities List is designed to be a resource for achieving just that!

When I met my clients Deborah and Shane, they were in a toleration relationship. They didn't actually have much conflict, but they certainly didn't have passion either. They made love once every six weeks or so, but it wasn't really satisfying to either one of them and sometimes it was easily a few months between times. I assigned them the Fun Activities List exercise and suddenly they found themselves laughing together more often, flirting as they hadn't in years, and really enjoying one another's company. This naturally led to more erotic energy between them and without any other efforts besides practicing curiosity, sharing honestly, and being kind, they went from each preferring to be on their own in the evenings to looking forward to being together at the end of each day.

Exercise

- Make a list of activities you enjoy doing together and have your partner do the same.

- Share your lists with each other. If you like things on your partner's list that weren't on your own, add them to your list. Your partner should do the same.

- Make a joint list which includes every activity that appears on both lists. Post the list where you will both see it regularly, such as your refrigerator or your bedroom wall. Make a point of doing activities on the list together once or twice a week.

CHAPTER 9
Who's Responsible?

G ood relationships are often viewed like negotiations, where both people need to give a little on each side in order to find a middle ground that works for everyone. Common attitudes and cliches include:

- You have to meet one another halfway or it will never work.

- A good relationship is where each person takes fifty percent of the responsibility.

- It takes two to tango!

While it definitely does take two to tango, one of the worst things you can do is to intentionally take fifty percent responsibility for the quality of your relationship. Consider this: In so many matters, it's the last few percentage points which distinguish the good from the outstanding, excellent, and world class levels of participation. Whether it's in science, Olympic sports, being chosen for the lead in a play, or really anywhere else, it's that last little bit, beyond two standard deviations from the mean, which distinguishes the most amazing from the rest of the pack.

In relationships it is no different. If you take fifty percent of the responsibility for how things feel in your relationship, and you expect your partner will take fifty percent too, believing that 50 +

50= 100, you will be disappointed. Because what is far more likely is that you will take fifty percent and he will take fifty percent but there will be some overlap in your focus. Inevitably the stickiest, most challenging and most important elements will be dropped. Taking one hundred percent responsibility for your relationship is key to its success. The absolute best relationships are born of both people taking one hundred percent responsibility for the quality of what they experience together.

What does it mean to take one hundred percent responsibility? That is an important, and also a somewhat elusive question. It is often simpler to see what *not* taking responsibility looks like. It's when you blame your partner for your own dissatisfaction. It's when you feel sorry for yourself, or for him, for being in the situation you are in. It's when you want him to change so *you* can feel differently. It's when you believe that the reason things are challenging is due to *his* inadequacies and when *he* fixes them, all will be well between you.

In contrast, taking full responsibility means looking at your part in creating the situation you are in. It doesn't absolve your partner from wrongdoing and a need to change, but it certainly doesn't mean you didn't contribute to creating the situation as well.

One of my favorite illustrations of how this works in real life is told by my friend and author Kristy Arnett. She and her husband Andrew had been married a number of years and at the time she was focused on her career as a writer and reporter, which required her to travel several months out of the year. The majority of her attention was on her career and consequently she had little energy left for her husband. With time, they had grown somewhat distant.

One day Kristy realized what was happening and (privately) decided she would revise her priorities. She committed to pulling back a little bit from her other activities in order to put more attention on her marriage. She was excited to reignite the intimacy, and stoke the passion with Andrew, whom she loved dearly. But when she shared this with Andrew, he pulled away in the exact opposite direction and admitted that he was contemplating divorce.

Confused and devastated, Kristy searched for answers about why her husband had a seemingly sudden change of heart. It was true that things hadn't been the best, but she herself had never considered divorce and he had never even hinted at it. In searching for answers, she discovered that he had recently begun an affair.

She was hurt, furious and filled with rage toward Andrew. Her heart was cracked apart. Her self-esteem plummeted. Yet despite it all, she still loved Andrew and was willing to work through it.

For months, they would seem to make progress, only to eventually find they had taken the same number or even more steps backwards. Then one day, in a conversation with a friend who also happened to be a life coach, Kristy detailed her and Andrew's latest argument. She complained that Andrew wasn't "committed enough". In response, her friend challenged Kristy to show her own commitment to fighting for her marriage with the simple act of writing on post-it notes. For thirty days, Kristy was to write something she loved or respected about Andrew, and leave the notes in places where he would read them.

Kristy was reeling inside. It angered her that she felt *she* had to express her appreciation and gratitude for this man who had betrayed her so deeply. Shouldn't *he* be doing this? After all, it was his fault that they were in this situation. But she had promised herself that she wouldn't leave Andrew until they had tried everything. Besides, Kristy is an action taker and it wasn't like her to turn down a challenge.

The notes were quite simple at first, admiring his smile and his commitment to excellence at work. A week and a half in, they fought and the argument remained unresolved. When it was time to write the next post-it, Kristy wanted to quit the challenge. With pen in hand she stared at the blank, square neon sheet of paper and it dawned on her what her friend was trying to show her: Kristy was committed until it got too hard. Then, she was one foot out the door, just like she was with this challenge. Maybe it wasn't Andrew who wasn't committed. Or perhaps Andrew's level of commitment was a reflection of Kristy's lack of it. That discovery shifted her attitude and she immediately wrote the most vulnerable message yet, acknowledging Andrew for loving her enough to stay and rebuild their marriage.

Day after day, she wrote. It was almost imperceptible at first, but slowly, the emotional wall between them began to dissolve. Each morning, Kristy made the conscious act of finding a specific thing she loved and respected about Andrew and each morning, Andrew felt loved and respected by her. A little more patience, empathy and kindness towards one another followed close behind, and Andrew began to feel safe confiding in Kristy and expressing his love again.

Kristy began to look forward to writing the notes and decided to extend the appreciation challenge to ninety days. As the days went on, her appreciation compounded, and she felt herself falling in love with Andrew again. They still had a lot of work to do, including sorting out the hurts and figuring out how to move forward in a way that aligned with a shared vision for their marriage. And they still needed to learn to forgive themselves and one another. But what really turned things around and showed them that transformation was possible, was Kristy writing those notes.

In the process of writing the notes, she shifted from a betrayed woman and a righteous victim, blaming Andrew for this terrible situation and wanting him to fix it, to taking action *herself*. She changed from knowing he should be treating her better to considering how she had contributed to what had happened and discovering how to show up as an empowered woman. She looked for how she could lean in and contribute everything in her power for the healing of their relationship. The results were undeniably successful. Many years later they are in love, committed, and wonderfully gratified with one another. This is what taking one hundred percent responsibility looks like in action.

The opposite of taking responsibility is being a victim, and from the time we are children, we all (unconsciously) learn how to be victims. It's a pattern we repeat again, and again, and again.

According to the victim triangle (a concept developed by Stephen Karpman MD and expanded on by Lynne Forrest) when we interact with other human beings without taking full responsibility for our own experience, we cope by taking on the roles of victim, persecutor or rescuer. Whereas fight, flight, freeze or faint is a description of an individual's response to her environment, the victim triangle is a relational model which provides an accounting for painful interactions between human beings.

Regardless of another person's intent, when we are hurt, we respond by embodying one of the three roles. When we respond by playing the victim, we consciously or unconsciously want sympathy, and hope that someone will take care of us. Alternatively, we may respond by becoming angry and aggressive, striking preemptively before anyone can hurt us again. This is what happens when the role of bully or persecutor is taken. The third possibility is that we feel hurt or stressed, and respond by taking care of others, rescuing them from the difficulty, and in so doing, feed our own ego. The full-blown expression of the rescuer is unbridled martyrdom, but it occurs frequently among mothers who prioritize everyone else's needs, and also among people who feel like others' problems are worse, so they ignore their own. Each of us definitely has one of the three roles as our main go-to response, but we embody any of them that suits us according to the context of a particular situation.

If you want to take one hundred percent responsibility for your own experience and be the one determining the quality of your relationship, it is essential to have awareness around your responses as victim, persecutor, or rescuer. All three are ways to avoid full personal responsibility. The main way out of the victim triangle is to observe your own internal reactivity and instead of acting on it, take responsibility for what is happening and change it. Some people refer to responsibility as the ability to respond, however, I would amend that to the ability to *choose* your response. The satisfaction, empowerment and sovereignty that comes with choosing to take on this level of responsibility is profound and markedly gratifying.

One of the most uncomplicated and straightforward ways of taking responsibility in your relationship is to implement the conclusions of research done by John Gottmann. He found that couples who are happy over the long term have a 5:1 ratio of affirming or complimentary statements to every critical one that is made. A critical statement includes pointing out ways your partner should be different from how he is currently behaving. It includes saying his way of being is irksome for you, that you don't like how he chews celery, or his tie clashes with his shirt, or you wish he would listen better, or it is so hard when he forgets things that are important for you, or he is unresponsive to your affection, or anything else that is not pleasurable for you.

Gottman's research doesn't imply you shouldn't say those things, but it does make clear that when you do you should also make a point of saying positive, affirming statements too, in the 5:1 ratio. State your gratitude for what a great provider he is. Or tell him how much you like his goofy sneakers, or the way he lightly brushes your hair off your face, or how you admire that he's never late for important meetings. Praise him for the warm-hearted and patient way he helps your kids with homework, or the way he is easy going about how intense your parents are, or anything else you experience with authentic gladness. Make sure to make a minimum of five positive statements for every one that is negative.

We all yearn to be seen and heard and recognized, whether the feeling is explicit or implicit. Whether it is effortless to express appreciation and acknowledgement of your spouse, or you need to deliberately choose to do so, sticking to the ratio is empowering and will be a huge win-win for your relationship.

In fact, when taking one hundred percent responsibility for the quality of your relationship, it is helpful to consider three distinct entities, namely you, your partner, and your union (the relationship you share).

In conscious partnership, wherein two adults are committed to growing together by cultivating curiosity, embracing honesty, being kind, and choosing happiness, and each of them aspires to take one hundred percent responsibility for the relationship, it is imperative that you tend to your own needs and take good care of yourself. Attending to your wants and desires, and being aware of your psychological, emotional, and bodily experience is essential when consciously determining the flavor of your interactions.

If you want your partner to change something in how he communicates with you or what he does, or how he touches or talks to you, by all means make your request. Do so with vulnerability and kindness. If he subsequently takes it personally, feels insulted, or has another complicated reaction, let it go. It is not your job to fix it. It's important to realize that taking responsibility is not about controlling a partner's response, it's about accepting it and aligning to it in a way that honors both of you.

Of course, it's important not to do anything meant to deliberately trigger him as that is not kind. But don't feel it's your job to patch anything up on the occasions he does have an emotional response as that would be attempting to manage his experience; it would be you taking on more of the burden of his experience than you allow him to hold, which is akin to mothering him. In this scenario you would be conveying that you need to nurture him because you don't believe he can handle his own emotional wellbeing on his own. In other words, it would be codependent.

There are times when you need to share something confronting for the health of your relationship, even though you know it will be hard for him to hear it. You correctly anticipate that his feelings will be hurt. However, he is your adult partner, not your child; you need to trust that he will find his way to handle his own emotional response. He may need to seek help in doing so from someone other than you, or perhaps he will request assistance from you. Either way, it's not up to you to do anything about it unless requested.

Any woman who is a nurturing caretaker is probably mothering her partner to some degree. Releasing this pattern is not easy. It will feel like giving up control in a way that creates massive uncertainty. Nevertheless it is necessary. The point here is to take one hundred percent responsibility for the quality of your relationship while simultaneously allowing your partner to do the same.

Exercise

- As you go through your day, keep a running tally of positive and negative comments you say to your partner. Do this for two days. Using positive language instead of negative language has benefits not only for your partner, but also for you!

- When you make a point of avoiding the trail of negativity and judgment, and instead focus on uplifting, appreciative thoughts and actions, you are quite likely to find yourself feeling more positive towards your partner, and feeling better about your life in general.

Typically, people are unconscious about just how often they make negative statements. For example, researchers found parents who love their children and are devoted to their wellbeing, make ninety-four negative comments to every six positive ones. People are often quite surprised to discover the number of times they are critical or negative without even noticing. The good news is that even a small amount of effort focused on turning negative and neutral comments into positive ones will have a wonderful impact on your relationships.

CHAPTER 10
Growth as the Basis for Relationship

W hether I am being interviewed on a podcast or by a journalist, or I am chatting with friends, I am often asked what my secret is. What's the secret sauce that allows Rodd and I to love one another so deeply. We have great, satisfying sex that continues to nourish, surprise, and inspire us. We continue to grow closer, all while raising four children, running a household, and pursuing our high stakes careers.

When I hear this question I respond with warm laughter, because there is no secret. There is not one single amazing thing we do. There is no technique or tool, or thing we say to one another, or specific communication style to account for it. The real answer is that the basis of our relationship is *growth* and it always has been. Growth is energizing and exciting.

We are devoted to our own growth and the growth of one another; we prioritize it individually and orient to it as the foundation for intimate relating and for stoking our passion. This means that, consistently, we are willing to make choices that prioritize our growth over everything else. We prioritize it over staying comfortable, over financial security, over fun, over appearances, and over the judgments of others.

We clearly understand that, beyond our love, what binds us is a lived commitment to our mutual ongoing development. We established this early in our relationship and have been completely aligned about it ever since. When we first got together, we had no idea that this would mean living in four different states, eight homes, raising four children, changing professions, plus a variety of other health-oriented decisions. Throughout the years, we have made numerous changes in our lifestyle as a result of valuing growth.

This also shows up in how we have prioritized educational opportunities over all other kinds of expenditures and any kinds of acquisitions. However, it definitely isn't necessary to make the same decisions we did in order to have the amazing benefits of a growth-based relationship. By definition it's going to look differently for every couple, and every individual. After all, each individual's learning will be particular to their personality, biography, and time of life, which in turn influences the journey for any two people in a partnership.

If one isn't living a growth based life, what's the alternative?

You may be familiar with the distinction between a fixed mindset and a growth-based mindset. Someone with a fixed mindset believes people are the way they are, and they will remain that way for the rest of their lives. They believe that there is nothing to be done about it other than dealing with it as best they can. In contrast, someone with a growth-based mindset believes that growth and transformation are *always* possible, and that there is always more to learn about who we are, how we think, and what motivates us. There are always more dreams and desires to discover and more opportunities to consider.

With a growth based mindset you experience wonderful times and you completely enjoy them ... while also looking for the learning in them. You might ask: What do I now know about myself and/or my husband that I didn't know before? What have I learned about life that I can now align with and integrate?

Similarly, when you are in challenging times, fighting a lot, in massive debt, feeling like nothing is turning out the way you want it to, or when you're dealing with a health crisis, you also look for the lessons. In every situation, strive to be present for what is happening. Instead of dissociating from reality, look for the learning and find the silver lining hidden inside the storm cloud. This does not mean denying tragedy, or overriding true devastation and grief, or anger and outrage. However, this does mean *feeling* what is real, being as authentic as possible, and leaning in to make friends with the experience.

Many aspirational teachers talk of the universal law, expressed as: "If you aren't growing then you are dying." In nature, there is no in-between. There is no neutral plateau. A tree is either growing, integrating nutrients, becoming stronger and more rooted, and moving toward the sunlight. Or it is decaying, beginning subtly, unseen by the naked eye at first and then progressing to highly visible phenomena with leaves fallen, crumbling insides, and bending branches unable to resist gravity's pull.

Given the options, I select growth. I simply follow the breadcrumbs of life while honoring my intuition. This way has taken me on a meandering path and I embrace it, respect it, and feel honored to be on it. I lean in as deeply and with as much courage as I can muster. I try to do this even when it's uncomfortable.

This polarity is true in relationships also. They *must* be growing in order for them to feel dynamic, energized, nourishing, comforting, and passionate. They must be growing to feel erotic energy, cultivate heat, and ooze with emotional intimacy. Without explicit or implied devotion to growth, relationships become stale. In that case, the toleration relationship is the best we can hope for. That is where growth within the relationship takes a back seat, and the front seat is filled with raising children, running the household, and common social priorities. Note that at first glance, growth in the relationship can be interwoven with raising children, and managing life together. It's certainly appropriate when babies are born, or when the deaths of dear friends and family members occur. But the really sustaining growth in a relationship, the foundational attitude described in this chapter, is one of growth explicitly focused on how you interact with one another. It is one where curiosity is cultivated, honesty embraced, happiness chosen, and where each of you continues to do all you can to take one hundred percent responsibility for the quality and expansion of your relationship.

People sometimes think of growth as relatively linear, like learning Math or English, riding a bike, or something else in which the focus is on the acquisition of skills. In emotional intelligence, personal growth, the deepening of relationships, as well as in the alchemical cauldron that *is* intimate relating, it is far more like a spiral. The first time around you hit a bump and really have a lot of work to do to get through it. Get through it you do, so you might think you are home free forever. But then, a few months or years, or sometimes even decades later, you find yourself experiencing the same challenges in your relationship. Again, you work it through, thinking now you have surely mastered it. But once again you find yourself in the same spot, albeit more aware, with the issue more refined and more nuanced than previously.

One of my greatest teachers in intimate relating is Harville Hendrix. My husband Rodd and I read his book *Getting the Love You Want* in 1998. We read it aloud and did the exercises together. Hendrix explains that we don't choose our partner for their positive qualities, we actually choose them for their "negative qualities." By negative qualities, he is referring to a partner's actions and ways of being which, as you become closer and more intimate, will inevitably trigger you. Trust your partner to be expert in activating your childhood wounds.

Invariably, even when partners have very different personalities than your parents, siblings and other influential people in your life, they end up behaving in ways that feel painfully familiar. The association with earlier experiences is often unconscious. Even so, this reactivation of childhood wounds can cause great pain and re-wounding with the absence of a growth based mindset. Or, in the context of a shared commitment to transformation, such activation provides exactly the experiences necessary to heal our wounds and catalyze us into the greatest, most powerful and most magnetic version of ourselves.

I believe that this very re-wounding, coupled with a fixed mindset, is the greatest contributor to the high divorce rate in the United States. Many people have accounted for the approximately fifty percent divorce rate in other ways. A few of the more well-known reasons include a lack of spiritual direction, female financial empowerment, and the challenges of living in a nuclear family without the support of a village. I don't dismiss any of these, but I also believe that modern marriage is an opportunity for growth, healing and transformation. We *will* be intensely activated by our partner. If we don't have the tools to recognize what's happening, heal, and then claim our sovereignty in the midst of the challenging feelings, the activation almost always feels re-traumatizing. The re-wounding evokes both past and current suffering, and therefore can become completely unbearable. In such circumstances, divorce seems to be the only solution to bring calm and a renewed sense of control over one's internal experience.

If you and your partner share a willingness to be present with one another even when it's hard, and you are committed to using tools to strengthen your sovereignty, then you get to create a different outcome. A common vocabulary for vulnerable honesty, an understanding of the importance of kindness, the means to increasingly take more responsibility for your own experience, and an increased capacity to nourish your union, provide the means to alchemize the activation of old wounds. That in itself is the foundational context for creating a passionate, erotically dynamic, attuned, supportive, hot, loving relationship. This book offers an invitation to that path, and I salute you for reading this far.

Devoting yourself to living a growth-based relationship will take you and your partner to realms you haven't even dreamed of going together. You will access physical, sexual, sensual, emotional, mental, and spiritual gratification, and your partner will too. In addition, you will find yourself with a smile behind your eyes, a sparkle in your step, and the ability to experience ecstasy and more creativity, in both your personal and professional lives.

Intimate relationships are *the* vehicle for personal transformation and a growth-based mindset is the requisite oxygen for making it happen.

Living a growth based relationship is also the most important step you can take for your family. What children need more than anything else is parents who know how to love one another (and have passionate sex together), as this is what creates an emotional legacy of infinite value.

Recently, a woman who loves and adores her man asked me a question. She was married once before and ultimately divorced because the passion died out and couldn't be revived, and she had enough self-respect to refuse to live that way. While she has been with her beloved for five years now, and their sex life is varied, soulful, and hot, she told me that she loves novelty. She has a fear that it will be impossible to continue to have new, exciting experiences during a lifelong partnership.

I *love* this question because it's honest, and points at something rarely discussed. Novelty in a long-term relationship is not the same as novelty while dating or in a new relationship. In both contexts there is always the possibility of role-play, kinky adventures, or similar means of creating novelty and that will appeal to some. But for busy professionals living full lives, novelty in long-term relationships usually comes through exquisite attention. It comes from touching one another with a depth of familiarity, devotion, and intentional focus that creates new, varied, and dynamic experiences. It comes with curiosity and asking a question in a new way that leads to revealing something that was never intentionally hidden but once shared feels like the key to understanding who your partner really is. More than toys, tools, and interesting positions, focused attention will take you to new heights and exquisite depths, to sensations and erotic communion previously unknown. This, of course, is only possible with someone you know well and with whom you share a growth-based relationship.

Exercise

All successful businesses have a vision statement which articulates the values and goals of the company. Most couples do not have something equivalent for their relationship. I believe that articulating your vision for conscious partnership is essential for growth. Collaboratively working through your values, goals, and the guiding principles for your relationship, creates an opportunity to both solidify and celebrate your lives in partnership.

87

Take your time with this exercise, and consider what you come up with to be a living document. I suggest you review it every year on your anniversary in order to reconnect with its essence and inspire renewed commitment to the values you share.

1. Write some short sentences that describe what you want in your relationship. Write all sentences in the present tense, in a positive form. (You should do this part separately from each other.)

Some examples:

· We are honest and vulnerable with one another.

· We have great sex.

· We make important financial decisions together.

· We are committed to our growth, both individually and as a couple.

Avoid sentences which blame or imply that one of you needs to change. Do not use negatives such as *We do not speak ill of each other.* Instead use a positive version of that same idea such as, *We speak highly of each other.*

2. Share your lists with each other and address any questions that arise. Underline any items on both of the lists which express the same idea even if you have used different words to describe them.

3. Create a master list which includes statements from both lists. If you each used different words to describe a similar idea, use words you can agree on to create a unified statement that resonates deeply for both of you.

4. If your partner lists something that you didn't include but you like having it there, and vice versa, include these too. For the purposes of this exercise, do not include anything in your vision statement that you have disagreements about.

5. Going forward, aspire to have your way of being, and the actions you take, align with your vision statement for conscious partnership. Do this while simultaneously enjoying the exquisite connection that results from trusting that the same will be true of your partner. It is a very powerful and generative experience to be on the same team, play by the same rules, and go for the same goals.

CHAPTER 11

Is Conscious Partnership for You?

M ost couples say they want a vibrant, passionate, sexy relationship and supportive, soulful communion with their partner. But those same couples are a lot less enthusiastic about committing to stretch and grow, and to doing what it takes to become whom they need to be in order to participate in such a relationship. Juicy, inspirational relationships are what most people want but few are willing to work towards. Why is that?

Well, in order to embody the six qualities of conscious partnership what is needed most of all is a growth mindset, and a willingness to shift how you show up in the world. Familiar ways of thinking, feeling, and acting are not going to suffice if you want to create a conscious partnership (or if you have one, take it to the next level). If the ways you operate within your current comfort zone were enough for such a transformation, you would already be experiencing the results you desire.

My clients are highly competent in most areas of life. They are professionally successful, sometimes extremely so, and they manage their family's needs with great care. When it comes to putting attention on their most intimate relationship, highly accomplished people often find it very challenging. They are out of practice being in the role of novice, however, to get the best results, they need to be willing to try new things. Feeling incompetent and hesitant, and taking risks like a clumsy beginner are part of the process. It's not possible to avoid this because transforming your relationship requires deep self-inquiry, and a willingness to be uncomfortable.

This takes a great deal of courage and when it's too confronting to the ego, some people shy away. It's not that their desire to experience a fantastic relationship diminishes, but their resistance to acquire new ways of relating wins out. Especially if you have done well in the world by being competent, organized, handling everything, and being in control of both yourself and your circumstances, surrendering to the unfamiliar can be excruciating. Conscious partnership is *not* a path of control; strategy will get you only so far.

Conscious partnership is the path of vulnerability, openhearted curiosity without assumption, and a willingness to say the things you most want to hide. It means facing what you have been hiding from yourself first, and then once excavated, sharing it with your partner. It is akin to learning to walk as a young child, because up-leveling your union requires the willingness to try new things despite knowing that they may not go well the first few times you try. Like a child learning to walk who falls down and gets back up again, it's essential to stick with it and try again no matter how awkward and uncomfortable it becomes. And all of this happens while you receive feedback from your partner about how well you are doing...

In practice, this is rather tricky because it can feel really dangerous. You may be telling yourself that your partner won't stick around if you share your innermost concerns and beliefs. Fear of abandonment, being hurt, or being judged, or fear of being "too much" is what keeps people from being vulnerable in the first place. These fears must be overridden in order to reveal the truth of who you are, and that is obviously no small feat. It requires courage, and surrender.

In committed relationships, an objective part of you knows that your partner will listen and do his best, even though it feels scary to you. But if your relationship is casual or in the process of ending, or there is some other reason you don't trust your partner, then stick to relatively more superficial truths when you share. Likewise, if your partner does not have your best interests at heart, consider carefully whether conscious partnership is even appropriate.

The Blueprint for Conscious Partnership is designed for couples who are fundamentally committed to their union. It takes courage and some people realize that and shy away. Motivated couples who stick with it and use the tools access profound results. They work to embody the six qualities of conscious partnership and are well rewarded for doing so. Some couples are excited to do this work and feel eager to have a teacher who will show them how. They want a guide to steer them through unfamiliar territory in order to assure the journey is successful.

Many different kinds of couples have transformed their relationships from toleration to nourishing, exciting, and connected. The tools work whether or not you are married, if you are heterosexual or gay, if you have been together for many decades or your relationship is still relatively young.

Are you currently in a relationship of toleration? Do you love your partner but feel more like roommates? Do you focus on your children or work in order to feel alive and motivated? Do you yearn to feel seen and heard by your partner? Do you yearn for more vibrancy and romance?

If so, the most gratifying, growth oriented, passionate opportunity is available through creating conscious partnership. Without it, you are essentially living without vitamins and minerals while hoping to be healthy.

Even if you decide it's perfectly okay for you to be unfulfilled, would you wish that for your children? They are the ones receiving your legacy of toleration and unmet yearning. You are training them to have the same lackluster relationship with the partners they choose in the future. Perhaps instead they won't have long relationships, in order to avoid feeling trapped. The only way to overcome the massive hurdles resulting from familial conditioning is intense inner work, so whatever you don't do will become their inheritance to deal with.

If you are tolerating your relationship, it is diminishing your sensuality and dampening your joy. It is also coloring how you experience yourself and the lens through which you interact with others. When you work on yourself in ways that are essential for experiencing conscious partnership, you transform. And when you transform so does everything, and everyone, around you.

In becoming the kind of woman who has a fantastic, passionate relationship, you access all kinds of other benefits as well. People who have great relationships have better health and live longer, make more money, and make love more often. According to the *Harvard Study of Adult Development* which tracked Harvard graduates over eighty years, the quality of your relationships at age fifty is a better indicator of your health at eighty than any other screening tool. Furthermore, it is also the *quality* of relationships, more than blood tests, genetics, social class, etc that determines happiness.

One of the best side effects of creating such a relationship is that you and you partner get to experience one another as your biggest fans. Imagine your partner coming home anticipating that you will be judgmental and critical of any new ideas he has. He will naturally take fewer risks and have less ambition, because his experience of your relationship will influence his choices. In contrast, when he knows that you are his biggest fan, that you will believe in him and support his dreams, he is far more likely to take risks at work and play bigger in life. The biggest gift you can give your partner is believing in his potential and being able to do so is one of the gifts of conscious partnership.

The same holds true for you. You will be more free and empowered to go for your own dreams when your partner knows how to be your biggest fan. Imagine daydreaming out loud and instead of him tuning out, or pointing out logistical and financial considerations, he is so attuned to you and your inner world, that he listens with curiosity and delight. When you doubt yourself, he is there, easily believing in you and reminding you of your brilliance. All of this is part of a conscious partnership.

In the Conscious Partnership Program, where I guide couples through this material using online teaching modules and coaching, participants get to witness other couples changing and evolving in amazing ways. Witnessing other couples face their issues is invariably encouraging, profoundly inspiring and highly motivational. It also provides an opportunity to learn from couples at various stages in their relationship. Some couples have been married for 25 years with children in college. Others have been married for 7 years and have young children at home. Others have been together for 18 months and want to create a solid foundation for their future. No matter the situation, practicing the six qualities of conscious partnership catalyzes profound transformation in everyone.

Embodying the six qualities of conscious partnership is not for the faint of heart because as you grow all your connections will inevitably evolve. Your relationship with your mother, your children, your coworkers, and everyone else in your life will improve. Initially it may be uncomfortable and awkward for the simple reason that any change can be disorienting. With time you'll find it invigorating and come to enjoy your expanded authenticity and newfound sovereignty.

When I look at the challenges we face today in the world at large, in the form of political breakdowns, violence, and diminishing civility, I dream of a time when a majority of couples are enjoying genuine, empowered, sexy, conscious partnerships. When that happens, those problems will dissolve or diminish, because our relationships determine how we experience the world and the quality of our contributions.

Exercise

Set aside time to write your responses to these questions:

1. What are the costs of keeping your relationship the way it has been up until now?

2. What are the benefits of creating a conscious partnership with your partner going forward?

95

CHAPTER 12
Make Your Dream Come True

Some people love to learn through reading and implementing the lessons. Others want the support and real-time guidance available through working with me. Either way, my mission is to make sure you know that you absolutely can have a long-lasting relationship with increasing emotional connection and sensual passion. Amazing, erotically charged, deeply satisfying sex is the natural consequence of increased presence, vitality, vulnerability, and sharing who you are. Learning to shed the pre-conditioned masks and behavioral patterns allows us to reconnect with our magnificent, authentic selves.

While it is often easier to see the way your partner disappoints you than to see your own contribution to the troubles in your relationship, in fact the best way to create the partnership you yearn for is to delve into your own individual work. Focus on becoming more aware of your internal processes and learn to be compassionate towards yourself. Actualize the six qualities of conscious partnership, and be vulnerable and courageous with your partner. Whether you feel unseen, unappreciated, taken for granted, wish he would take more care with you, or anything else that has you feeling dissatisfied and unfulfilled, the more *you* *t*ake responsibility for how you feel, the more open and genuine your connection with your partner will be.

96

Each of the chapters in *Uncompromising Intimacy* contains insights and guidance which will have an immediate impact in your life. When you choose to lean in and embody all six essential qualities of conscious partnership, the results will last a lifetime and continue, like a fine wine, to improve with age.

The journey begins with celebrating your love, remembering why you are together with your partner and what had you say yes to sharing your life with him. If you have been feeling frustrated with him, gratitude and celebrating your love are the first steps to opening your heart.

It's also important to forgive yourself, knowing you are influenced by your childhood role models and the societal messages that go deep into our psyches. In traditional Fijian culture, "You've gained weight" was a compliment. Girls in Fiji loved to hear it. In 1995, television programming was brought to the island for the first time. With it came images of slender actresses and familiar messages about body shame. Just three years later, in 1998, teenage girls in Fiji had shifted into describing themselves as ugly, fat and overweight. This example provides a small window into how large the influence of media, society, and our familial role models is on how we think and behave. They are hugely significant in determining our attitudes about who we are.

In Western culture the media, society, and our familial role models give us messages about delusional fairy tale relationships, coupled with memes about divorce and marital dissatisfaction. Among couples who stay together, most are in toxic, termination, or toleration relationships. It's important to understand that this has influenced you; it's also essential to seek out other experiences. Learn from growth minded communities and befriend other couples who are creating conscious partnerships. (The Conscious

Partnership Program is a group program for just this reason—couples who enroll connect with others on the same path.)

Once you acknowledge your personal and societal context, and you evoke what drew you together, then share what you appreciate about one another. Next, focus on cultivating curiosity. Ask open ended questions and gladly receive any responses given. It's important that you affirm the sharing and that you don't respond negatively to any content. The goal is to cultivate curiosity and integrate it into the culture of your relationship.

In the process, you are sure to become more curious about yourself and your own responses as well. As you see yourself and your partner anew, share what you are discovering. Also express anything you may have previously avoided saying. Start with more benign revelations and use the three-part method of speaking your truth by asking if your partner is available, stating why you are sharing, and naming the outcome you desire for both of you. As you and your partner become more comfortable with speaking in this way, it will provide a solid foundation for you to communicate about more personal, edgy, and vulnerable topics.

It's vital to communicate anything you have been avoiding because if you are withholding in the emotional realm, you will be withholding sexually too. As my client Rachel so aptly put it, "Being vulnerable in one area helped us open up in sex as well. Guarding ourselves emotionally made us guarded in sex."

Once you are in the habit of sharing honestly, being kind in your communications becomes paramount. In fact, while I write about each separately for ease of intellectual access, they are inextricably intertwined. Making progress in sharing honestly necessitates progress in being kind and vice versa.

Being kind is largely achieved through a warm and softer tone, rather than a harsh, critical or disconnected one. It is also in direct contrast to being nice (where you prioritize others' needs as you perceive them) and being self-centered (where you focus solely on your own needs.)

The skills you develop in communicating with your partner will help you in any challenging relationship.

Savannah shared this with me:

> "I took Alexandra's advice for couples, to state your intention and goals before engaging in difficult conversations, and I applied it when communicating with my stepchildren. It has completely transformed the way they receive what I say. Instead of them immediately feeling provoked and responding with confusion, anger, hurt, and resentment, they now open up and really *listen* to what I say. Alexandra's technique created a subtle shift in communication which has brought the long-awaited recalibration of our previously trying relationship. We have made real progress toward something new and trustworthy. Most surprisingly, and completely unexpected, my stepchildren have started implementing this kind of respectful communication style when they speak amongst themselves, to me, to their Dad, and with others. I'm thrilled!"

Building on the foundation of cultivating curiosity, embracing honesty, and being kind, you will be well positioned to consider whether you want to choose happiness. Internally pivoting toward happiness entails evolving from a win/lose dynamic with your partner, to a win/win for both of you.

In each of these qualities of conscious partnership, you learn how to take responsibility for the quality of your relationship. You understand that relationships are not fifty-fifty endeavors. For your relationship to be everything you want it to be ... and more ... it is key that you take one hundred percent responsibility for yourself, your emotions, your communication style and the quality of your union. This means you don't look to your partner to do something to make you feel better, as a way to rescue you from how you feel. And on the flip side, you don't aim to control or rescue how he feels either.

The singular variable which is essential in conscious partnership is the commitment to seek growth. Whereas a fixed mindset accepts that people are how they are, that your relationship is how it is, and nothing can be fundamentally changed, having a growth mindset means knowing that healing and transformation are always possible. Choosing a growth mindset and creating a vision for your conscious partnership which honors your and your partner's devotion (to your own and one another's growth) is the foundation for erotic satisfaction and lifelong passionate lovemaking.

As you read these final sentences, my wish for you is that you have already experienced significant shifts in perspective and that you have begun to reorient your relationship with new insights and hope. I trust that it is just the beginning of a lifetime of practice and delight. The magnificence in the six qualities of conscious partnership are that they provide the means to emotional intimacy and hot, passionate, deeply satisfying sex, which gets better and better all the time. Please know, there is always more to discover in yourself and in your partner and knowing how to do this *without* compromising is the key to a fantastic relationship.

Imagine a world where, instead of postponing marriage and avoiding commitment, or going for it while knowing there's a statistically strong likelihood that you will get divorced, you look around and see couples deeply in love and continuing to grow. They have energy to honor themselves and one another. They are fluent in vulnerability, humility, and the sovereignty that comes from whole body happiness. And they generously share who they truly are with one another.

Imagine children growing up in a world where people have the ability to be attentive to each other, where authentic connection is prevalent and thus the incidence of violence, addiction, mental health issues and other societal challenges are diminished or even eradicated. Instead, inclusion, respect, and hope are the norm for all.

In addition to any way you already endeavor to improve life on earth, transforming your relationship will definitely expand love and peace in your family and in society at large.

Acknowledgments

I acknowledge my mother, and my father. I learned so much from what did and mostly what didn't work in your marriage, and in your subsequent marriages as well. I never could have said it this way as a child, but you really taught me that love is essential and definitely not enough to create a joyful, long lasting marriage. The legacy you gave me inspired me to learn how to create a different legacy for my family and I am grateful for everything needed for that to happen.

Thank you to my many clients who have taught me so much about relationships and what it takes to improve them in delicious, sustainable ways. I won't mention you by name, but if you have been coached by me at any time in my career, or if you were a patient who sought medical advice that included navigating what arose in your familial relationships, know that you have contributed to this book.

I am grateful for my coach, mentor, and friend, Marla Mattenson and her partner Julian Colker. Thank you for seeing me better than I could see myself, and for holding me so exquisitely, such that I learned how to impact others on a far larger scale than I knew to dream of. Thank you for blending love, precision, and creativity in your teachings and assignments. And thank you for giving me an embodied experience of what generosity and collaboration feels like. You know that a lot of what is in this book is material you shared with me, encouraging me to truly make it my own and then share it with others. Your beaming smile and expanded affirmation in this has been profoundly encouraging.

Thank you to my business partner Ryan Carter, for getting me, for perceiving my message, knowing the world needs to hear it, and choosing to partner with me so that millions of people can improve the quality of their relationships. Thank you too for your contributions to making this book excellent. I love that our visions are aligned and that we will serve many with the use of our complementary skill sets.

Thank you to Dr. Angela Lauria, and her team including Cheyenne Giesecke, Ora North, Emily Tuttle, and Ramses Rodriguez for creating a strong container with the right amount of direction and open-endedness for me to share my message. Thank you for creating systems and instruction that feel personal, relevant, and completely encouraging. There is no question this book would not have been written without the path you have forged and the warm welcome to me as I chose to walk down it.

Thank you also to Barrie Cole, wordsmith extraordinaire, for your belief in me and for assisting me in crossing the finish line. You went above and beyond to bring a previously missing coherence. I am immensely grateful.

I'm not sure I would have been motivated to do the hard and gratifying work of transformation were it not for the inspiration and uncensored feedback I receive from my children:

Josephine, your radiance and warm, joyful presence has always been one of my greatest sources of inspiration. I am so grateful for your interest and active support of my work as a relationship coach. (And I love when you call your mama to get free coaching!)

Christopher, your perceptive abilities and high standards in communication have been a profound invitation to deepen my authenticity and learn to relate in a warm, casual way.

Gabriel, you *always* know what the emotional truth of the matter is. I love the kind, caring, nurturing, curious way you move through life.

Jacob, you were with us a short time, yet your impact is forever.

Matthew, your capacity for love and affection has opened my heart, and nourishes it daily.

And last, but not ever least, to my incredible husband Rodd. Thank you for always being devoted to a growth based marriage even when we had no idea what that would mean. Thank you for continuing to grow yourself, to insightfully support my growth, and to co-create our Union so it continues to become ever more magnificent. Your inner stance makes each day an invitation to deepen our connection and grow our bliss. And thank you for being so willing to have me share how we do it with anyone who reads this book. I love you.

About the Author

Alexandra Stockwell, MD is a Physician turned Relationship and Intimacy Expert who is known as *The Relationship Catalyst* and the creator of the Conscious Partnership Program. She believes the key to passion, fulfillment, and intimacy isn't compromise--it's being unwilling to compromise.

A wife of 24 years and mother of four, Alexandra guides men and women towards the freedom to be themselves, because it's when we feel loved for who we are that our relationships become juicy, nourishing, and deeply satisfying.

Through Conscious Partnerships, Alexandra helps couples infuse pleasure and purpose into all aspects of life—from the daily grind of running a household, to clear and intimate communication, to ecstatic experiences in the bedroom!

Thank You

Congratulations and thank you for completing this book. I hope you take what you've learned here into your relationship and use it to create more emotional intimacy and sensual passion with your partner.

If you enjoyed this book and found its contents valuable, I would love to continue guiding you along the path of creating the relationship you desire.

I've created an on-demand training that dives deeper into the concepts outlined in these pages and introduces new concepts I wasn't able to fit in the book. This training is my gift to you as a way to say thank you for purchasing this book.

To register for your free copy of this training just visit:
www.AlexandraStockwell.com/6Steps

Please send any comments, questions or edits to:
www.Alexandrastockwell.com/Contact

Wishing you much fun and delight with your partner,

With Love,
Alexandra